ERIE'S
BACKYARD
STRANGLER

ERIE'S BACKYARD STRANGLER

TERROR IN THE 1960s

JUSTIN DOMBROWSKI

THE
History
PRESS

Published by The History Press
Charleston, SC
www.historypress.com

Copyright © 2023 by Justin Dombrowski
All rights reserved

First published 2023

Manufactured in the United States

ISBN 9781467153485

Library of Congress Control Number: 2022947159

This book is dedicated to

Laura Mutch
Clara Carrig
Helen Knost
Eleanor Free
Nancy Wierzbicki
Mary Lynn Crotty
Davida Boyer
Marian Graham

and to those who remain unknown, with justice delayed.

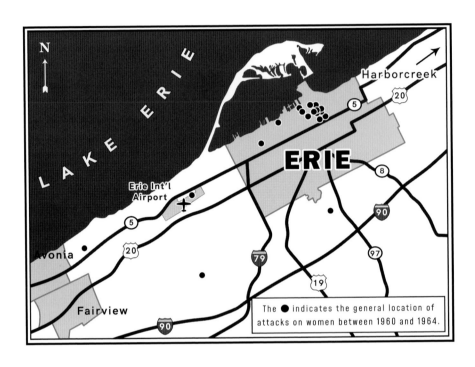

The ● indicates the general location of attacks on women between 1960 and 1964.

CONTENTS

ACKNOWLEDGEMENTS

This book, like any other, had its challenges and roadblocks, especially given its extensive research. From the beginning, my acquisitions editor, J. Banks Smither, was on board and provided his support, and without his input and direction, this book could not have been possible.

Various family members of the victims within this book have reached out to offer support and encouragement since this project began. One of those individuals, Valerie Kocher, was kind enough to give permission for the use of the photograph of Laura Mutch that appears in this book.

Chief court reporter Sonya Hoffman and her staff were instrumental in locating and reproducing trial transcripts utilized in my research into the trials against Daniel Biebighauser and John Howard Willman. Their promptness and professionalism were greatly appreciated.

As always, the staff at the Erie County Historical Society at the Hagen History Center provided immense help. Whether it involved sifting through thousands of photographs or pinpointing locations long gone, their assistance helped breathe life into this story, allowing me to take the reader back to Erie in the 1960s.

The staff of the Fairview Area Historical Society were also kind, courteous and knowledgeable in their expertise in being able to pinpoint areas of interest beyond the Erie City limits that have been long lost.

John L. Scott Sr. is a staple in Erie as far as aerial historical photographs go, and he was generous enough to grant permission for the use of the photograph of West Erie Plaza in the 1950s.

The staff at the Pennsylvania State Archives also provided considerable assistance that cannot go unacknowledged.

The staff at the Boston Public Library were both courteous and helpful in tracking down information about George Frazier and providing copies of his column "The Quiet Ones," which detailed his stay in Erie around the time Lynn Crotty was murdered.

I am grateful for the assistance of my friends Justin Schnars and Brandon Rizzonelli in accompanying me on numerous "field trips" to the scenes of the attacks and murders listed in this book. Steve Towns and Nancy Parish-Towns were both generous and crucial in reviewing one of many numerous drafts of this book.

As with *Murder & Mayhem in Erie, Pennsylvania*, my father, Gary Dombrowski, once again helped assist with the maps within this book. My mother, Julie, continued to provide her daily support and encouragement.

Over the past few months, I have received immeasurable support from friends, colleagues and family members. Finally, this book could not have been possible without the support of my children, Sierra, Sophia and Benjamin, and my wife, Sara, who always selflessly provided their love, support and understanding.

PREFACE

I mmediately following the completion of *Murder & Mayhem in Erie, Pennsylvania*, I began discussing plans with The History Press for my next project. After several back-and-forth discussions, those plans materialized as something entirely different, with my next book focusing on a stand-alone tale of local true crime. Although I loved the opportunity to dissect and present tales of murder and mayhem from Erie's long-forgotten past in my first book, I was looking for something more challenging.

This book proved to be just that.

Erie's Backyard Strangler encapsulates several cases that occurred in Erie, Pennsylvania, from the fall of 1960 until 1964. During this time, Erie experienced an epidemic of attacks against women, ranging from assaults to rapes and murders. Investigators believed that the crimes during this period were connected. Some cases appeared similar, while others, as bizarre as they were, seemed isolated from the others. Some of the cases in this book remain unsolved, with others resulting in convictions that placed those responsible behind bars.

As for the crimes, whether or not they were connected and who was ultimately responsible or not responsible—this is left up to the reader to draw their own conclusions.

During the 1960s, pulp magazines provided sensationalized and macabre content for aficionados of true crime. In Erie, crimes that occurred there during this period were magnets for those publications, which in turn provided some material for this book. Some of these articles included "The Pennsylvania Killer-Rapist Wore Ladies' Undies," by Harold Whitby, for the January 1969 issue of *Official Detective Stories*. In writing the article, Whitby used information from *Erie Daily Times* reporters Lester A. Lowman and Ralph "Bat" Humble. Despite Lowman's untimely death in 1967, his notes and research, some never revealed to the public, corroborated details that were found to be genuine.

Additional information came from both *True Detective Magazine* and *Front Page Detective*. As is common in such periodicals, these articles contained altered dates and pseudonyms surrounding the events of the crimes themselves, for both dramatic and legal purposes.

Despite the fact that these crimes occurred over sixty years ago, there was no direct access to files within the City of Erie Police Department, Millcreek Police Department and Pennsylvania State Police. In Pennsylvania, strict laws protect these criminal investigations from the general public, which, in turn, can be costly in FOIA request fees and, additionally, take years to complete.

My primary sources of information were both the *Erie Daily Times* and the *Erie Morning News*; several hundred of their articles were instrumental in helping craft the narrative for this book. Additional information comes from over 2,282 pages of court transcripts, including the cases of *Commonwealth v. Willman*—for both trials, in 1964 and 1968—which amounted to 1,214 pages. *Commonwealth v. Biebighauser*, consisting of 1,068 pages, also contained crucial information about the murder of Mary Lynn Crotty. These transcripts provided firsthand accounts, dialogue and excerpts from autopsy reports.

Although there was much information to utilize in writing this book, one needs to be cognizant of the challenges of investigating these crimes, which occurred a long time ago. Not all crimes against women in Erie during this time were reported to police. By the 1960s, law enforcement had made tremendous strides in the way it conducted investigations since the early 1900s; however, this was still well before the introduction of DNA and forensics, which helped shape how we investigate crimes today.

Finally, this being a work of narrative nonfiction, anything appearing between quotation marks is from the sources described within this introduction. This allowed me to utilize the limited space and word count to provide the story as it was meant to be told.

During the 1960s, Erie was still experiencing continued growth post–World War II, with its manufacturing and fishing industries providing thousands of jobs to those who resided in the Gem City. Set during this decade, known as "the years that changed America," this book tells of the failures and successes of those forever connected to these crimes that occurred during a time that forever changed the city of Erie—a time, as *Boston Herald* columnist George Frazier wrote when visiting the city in 1963, when Erie was "a town that never seems not touched by terror and tragedy."

DRAMATIS PERSONAE

The story of Erie's Backyard Strangler involves many individuals who were connected to the investigation between 1960 and 1968. Whether they be law enforcement, victims, reporters, attorneys, judges or suspects, those mentioned prominently within the text are listed here, in order of their appearance in the story, with a brief synopsis of who they were and the role they played. Some names have been changed to protect individuals' identities under certain circumstances.

Chester "Wizzy" Wizikowski
Detective sergeant, City of Erie Police Department

Raymond J. Lapenz
Detective sergeant, City of Erie Police Department

Laura Mutch
Victim, murdered on December 30, 1960; her body was found the following morning behind 717 Holland Street

Charlotte Clugh
Witness who found Laura Mutch's body behind 717 Holland Street on the morning of December 31, 1960

Phillip Lupo
Detective, City of Erie Police Department

Carl Malinowski
Detective sergeant, City of Erie Police Department

Armand Chimenti
Detective captain, City of Erie Police Department

Carl Kalinowski
Sergeant of identification, Detective Bureau, City of Erie Police Department

George Meucci
Son of murder victim Laura Mutch

Merle E. Wood
Coroner, Erie County

Dr. John A. Fust
Pathologist, Hamot Hospital

Herbert J. Johnson Jr.
Erie County district attorney, 1955–63

Robert Ross
Detective sergeant, City of Erie Police Department

The Reverend Richard J. Gibbons
Pastor, Gospel Tabernacle Church; one of the last persons who saw Laura Mutch alive the night she was murdered

William Nevin
Lieutenant, Pennsylvania State Police; lie detector expert responsible for testing suspects in the beginning of the Mutch investigation

Edward Williams
Chief of police, City of Erie Police Department, 1954–62

Roy Mong
Chief county detective, Erie County District Attorney's Office

Frank Figaski
Detective inspector, City of Erie Police Department

Betty Quick
Victim, attacked on February 28, 1961, in a field near the 2000 block of East Eleventh Street

Clara Carrig
Victim, sexually assaulted and stabbed at her residence, 621 East Sixth Street, on June 2, 1961

Thomas Carrig
Husband of Clara Carrig

Maurice Sheehan
Detective sergeant, City of Erie Police Department

Hugh "Red" Barr
Columnist, *Erie Daily Times*

Richard Worlund
Arsonist who set fire to several apartment complexes in Erie on July 5, 1961; briefly a suspect in the Mutch and Carrig cases

George H. Radaker
Chief of police, City of Erie Police Department, 1962–66

Helen Knost
Victim, abducted from West Erie Plaza on July 20, 1962; assaulted and her throat slit before being abandoned in Fairview

Tyco Lange
Detective, Pennsylvania State Police

Leo Weir
Detective, Pennsylvania State Police

James Moore
Convicted sex offender and murderer, briefly suspected of attacking Helen Knost

Margaret Renz
Neighbor and friend of Eleanor Free

Eleanor Free
Victim, found bound and strangled inside her bedroom in her residence, 1018 Washington Place, on December 17, 1962

James Free
Estranged husband of Eleanor Free

Clifford Salow
Acquaintance of Eleanor Free who sent endearing postcards to Free, signed "Mr. X"; considered the prime suspect in her murder

Frank W. Lesch
Corporal, Pennsylvania State Police; administered lie detector examinations in the Free murder investigation

Chester J. Miller
Deputy chief, City of Erie Police Department

Lewis Penman
Detective sergeant, Pennsylvania State Police

Mary Lynn Crotty
Victim, raped and strangled on January 21, 1963, and dumped in Ax Murder Hollow

John Floyd Harvey
Coworker of Daniel Roy Biebighauser

Paulette Cywinski
Friend and classmate of Mary Lynn Crotty

Daniel Roy Biebighauser
Convicted of murdering Mary Lynn Crotty; briefly suspected of the murder of Laura Mutch and attacks on Helen Knost and Clara Carrig

Edward Strong
Sergeant, Lawrence Park Police Department

Nancy Wierzbicki
Victim, attacked by Daniel Biebighauser on December 3, 1962; Nancy's real name has been changed to protect her identity

George Frazier
Columnist, the *Boston Herald*

Louise Biebighauser
Wife of Daniel Biebighauser

Beverly Biebighauser
Mother of Daniel Biebighauser

Davida Boyer
Victim, assaulted on July 6, 1963, after accepting a ride from the Tally Ho Bar

Sophie Gorchinsky
Witness, 235 East Front Street; saw the aftermath of the altercation between Davida Boyer and her attacker

Ann Kopes
Witness, 217 East Front Street; witness to events the night Davida Boyer was attacked

William Serafini
Patrolman, City of Erie Police Department

Thomas Stanton
Detective sergeant, City of Erie Police Department

Irene Fogle
Waitress at the Tally Ho Bar the night of July 5, 1963; saw Davida Boyer leaving with the man who attacked her

Michael Snider
Detective sergeant, City of Erie Police Department

Charles McCurdy
Detective sergeant, City of Erie Police Department

Melvin Swanson
Detective sergeant, City of Erie Police Department

John Howard Willman
Truck driver, arrested for the attack on Davida Boyer; later confessed to the murder of Laura Mutch

Paul J. DeDionisio
Captain, City of Erie Police Department

Richard V. Scarpitti
Erie County district attorney, 1963

Michael J. Kinecki
Alderman, Second Ward

Harry R. Willman
Brother of John Willman

Catherine Willman
Sister-in-law of John Willman, married to John's brother Harry

Eugene "Gene" Willman
Brother of John Willman

Carol Willman
Sister-in-law of John Willman; married to John's brother Eugene

Dr. Frank J. Pizzat
Clinical psychologist, examined John Willman in the fall of 1963 on behalf of the Erie County District Attorney's Office

Dr. Michael F. Cleary
Psychiatrist, hired by defense attorneys to examine John Willman

Edward H. Carney
Erie County district attorney, 1964–65; later served as Erie County common pleas judge

Bernard F. Quinn
Attorney, defended John Willman in 1964

James E. Beveridge
Attorney, defended John Willman in 1964

John M. Wolford
Attorney, hired by the ACLU to be present during John Willman's preliminary hearing

Edmund Woolslayer
Truck driver, found the body of Marian Graham

Marian E. Graham
Victim, found nude and murdered on January 30, 1964, in a grove located off of Glenwood Park Avenue

Ralph William Rogers
Unemployed welder, suspect in the Helen Knost attack and convicted of the murder of Marian Graham

Elmer L. Evans
Judge, Erie County Court of Common Pleas

Lindley R. McClelland
Judge, Erie County Court of Common Pleas; served as district attorney 1966–67

Richard F. Brabender
Attorney, appointed special prosecutor by District Attorney William E. Pfadt to prosecute Willman's retrial in 1968

Michael Palmisano
Assistant district attorney, Erie County

Vedder J. White
Attorney, helped assist Willman's defense for his retrial in 1968

Dana "Sher" Sherwood Jones
Erie County public defender

Will J. Schaaf
Attorney, helped assist Willman's defense for his retrial in 1968

Chapter 1

HOLLAND STREET HORROR

I t was just past four o'clock in the morning on December 31, 1960, as forty-year-old George Meucci stood before the front desk of the City of Erie Police Department in the basement of city hall. Outside, a cool breeze rattled the frost-covered windows. Across from him, Detective Sergeant Carl Kalinowski feverishly scribbled back and forth, filling in a missing persons report.

Kalinowski paused, looking up at Meucci.

"Haven't I seen you before?" Kalinowski gestured with his pencil. "Weren't you in here only a week or so ago to tell us about another missing person?"

"That was my brother Leonard Mutch Jr.," Meucci mumbled.

"And now you want to report your mother missing?"

Meucci glumly nodded, telling Kalinowski that his mother, sixty-year-old Laura Mutch, was still grieving the death of his brother Leonard and that as a religious woman had recently found solace in prayer. The night prior, around seven o'clock, Meucci dropped her off at the Full Gospel Tabernacle Church, located at 560 East Eighth Street, near the corner of Ash Street. Before driving away, Meucci attempted to get his mother to accept a ride home, but she declined, preferring to walk instead.

Around three o'clock in the morning, Meucci received a phone call telling him his mother never returned home. Hastily dressing himself, Meucci walked to his parents' home at 615 Holland Street. From there, he and his brother Andrew searched the neighborhood for their mother. It was only after speaking with the pastor of the Full Gospel Tabernacle

Church, the Reverend Richard J. Gibbons, that the family decided to file a missing persons report.

Meucci described his mother as heavyset with graying hair and blue eyes. When he last saw her, she was wearing a heavy pink overcoat over a navy blue dress, her head covered with a flower-patterned scarf.

Kalinowski looked over the report. Having been with the department for the past five years, he knew it was not out of the ordinary to receive missing persons reports such as this. There was, however, a peculiarity about the report that nagged at him. Next, Kalinowski placed a call to Detective Captain Armand Chimenti. The year 1960 was drawing to a close, and detectives were being kept busy investigating dozens of burglaries, purse snatchings and assaults in the city's east side neighborhoods.

Kalinowski watched Meucci shuffle out of the department. He hoped George Meucci's mother would be found—and soon.

A cold front continued to hammer the lakeshore, and temperatures had dipped near below zero when Detective Sergeants Chester "Wizzy" Wizikowski and Raymond J. Lapenz were tasked with searching for Laura Mutch. The pair traversed several different routes Mutch could have traveled on her way home. As they patrolled the dark streets and alleys around East Eighth Street, the detectives also ventured into nearby all-night restaurants and diners, thinking Mutch may have had an accident or wandered in for a late-night cup of coffee. Wizikowski and Lapenz came up empty-handed.

As the crisp wind howled and the dark blue sky gave way to the morning twilight on the horizon, the detectives were unable to locate any trace of Laura Mutch.

Laura Mutch had simply vanished.

Hours later, just before nine o'clock in the morning, thirty-seven-year-old Charlotte Clugh had just finished feeding her children inside their small duplex located on the first floor of 717 Holland Street. Making her way to her bedroom at the rear of the duplex, Clugh tidied up, preparing to leave for an appointment that morning at the Boston Store.

Raising the shade of her window, Clugh was met with a grisly sight.

Below the window was the body of an elderly woman lying on her back, hands at her sides, her dress appearing to have been lifted and bunched around her waist. The woman's eyes were open, her mouth slackened wide, and something had been shoved into her mouth.

Frightened, Clugh brought her hand to her mouth.

"Oh, my God," Clugh muttered, her voice quivering.

Detective Sergeants Chester Wizikowski and Raymond Lapenz. *Erie Daily Times.*

"Momma, what's wrong?" asked her son, Frank, who was standing in the doorway.

"Nothing," Clugh stammered as she dropped the shade.

Clugh brushed past her son, rushing to the front door. Turning to her son as she opened the door, Clugh slithered her arms into the sleeves of her coat, telling Frank to make sure his siblings stayed inside and to not go near the back of the house.

Clugh stepped out into the piercing cold, trudging her way next door to the Muffler King building at 202 East Eighth Street, where she told her landlord of the frightening discovery.

Clugh's landlord immediately phoned the switchboard operator at police headquarters.

At the same time Charlotte Clugh made the gruesome discovery in her backyard, Detective Sergeant Carl Malinowski was sipping his cup of

Top: 717 Holland Street on the morning of December 31, 1960. *Erie Times News*.

Bottom: Witness Charlotte Clugh poses in the backyard of 717 Holland Street. *Erie Times News*.

coffee at Jim and Lee's restaurant. Standing just over six feet tall, the husky, fifty-seven-year-old detective was an Erie native, like most of those in the department. Malinowski had worked as a salesman and driver for the Erie County Milk Association and often operated a small barbershop from his home. In 1936, he attended the state police school, followed by the FBI school in Erie in 1939. After joining the police department, Malinowski served as a street sergeant and patrol sergeant, and since 1949, he had served as a detective sergeant.

Sitting next to Malinowski was his partner, fifty-two-year-old Detective Philip Lupo. Lupo was a Baltimore native but had spent most of his life in Erie. Following World War II, in which Lupo served as a lieutenant, he joined the police department in Erie.

As both men settled into their cups of coffee, they received a call over the radio about the discovery of the body behind 717 Holland Street. Malinowski stood up, fishing some bills from his pocket and leaving them on the counter as he made his way to a nearby phone to notify Captain Chimenti. Within minutes, both detectives peeled away from the curb, en route to the scene.

Minutes later, Lupo and Malinowski arrived on scene, greeted by a small crowd of men and women clustered in front of 717 Holland. Sergeant Robert Sheridan and Officers Paul Miller and Raymond Pelkowski, having just arrived minutes prior, greeted the detectives, directing them toward the backyard. As the detectives walked along the northern side of the building, their feet crunching against the ice, they entered through the narrow, three-foot-wide clearance between the duplex and the neighboring garage of the Konzel Construction Company.

As they rounded the corner, the body came into view underneath the rear bedroom window. Morning frost clung to their nostrils as they inched closer, their own breathing drowned out by the distant barking of a dog in the morning sun. Inspecting the body more closely, they noticed one of the woman's shoes was partially off, the other still on her foot. Her coat was open, and her blue dress underneath was pushed up to and around her hips, leaving the victim nude from the waist down. Near her right hand lay a black Bible. Two feet from the Bible were a pair of women's glasses, with the right lens broken.

Detective Lupo crouched down on the ground, eyeing several buttons nearby that looked as if they had been torn from the woman's coat and sweater. Malinowski's attention was frozen on a flower-patterned scarf, which had been elaborately tied around the woman's throat and mouth.

Leaning over, Malinowski noted that the woman's neck was bruised and swollen and that the scarf had been tied and knotted in an intricate way. Soon, the detectives were joined by Detective Captain Armand Chimenti and Sergeant of Identification Carl Kalinowski.

Chimenti, the son of Italian immigrants, had spent time in his twenties working at the Erie Dock Company at the foot of Parade Street before going on to graduate from the FBI Academy and join the police department in Erie, where he rose through the ranks. With an infectious smile and chiseled good looks, Chimenti was an all-around gentleman who gained the respect of those he worked with as well as the general public. Kalinowski, who arrived with Chimenti that morning, armed with his speed graphic camera, was filling in for duties normally performed by Inspector Frank Figaski, who was at home nursing a sprained right ankle.

As Chimenti and Kalinowski looked on, Lupo pointed out the buttons. Kalinowski stepped forward, carefully placing them into evidence envelopes. One of the detectives also pointed out what appeared to be an unidentified liquid substance on the ground near Konzel's garage.

It was just past nine thirty in the morning when Sergeant Kalinowski began photographing the scene. As detectives searched the backyard, they realized there was very little evidence visible. The ground was frozen, with no recent snowfall that would be able to reveal any fresh footprints. There was also no evidence of any weapons. Toward the rear of the yard, detectives sifted through several discarded Christmas trees, one of which had blown into the alley near the Hill Mill Dairy building, but nothing of additional value was located.

By then, an ambulance had arrived with an intern, Dr. Morris, from Hamot Hospital, and the woman was officially pronounced deceased. Additional patrolmen and detectives fanned out to the nearby streets and alleyways, searching for additional evidence and questioning neighbors. The search proved fruitless, save for a frozen footprint found in ice behind the Pennsylvania Rubber Company near East Seventh Street.

Chimenti, Kalinowski, Lupo and Malinowski were still in the rear of 717 Holland when Erie County coroner Merle E. Wood arrived on scene. Wood, thirty-one, was wrapping up his first year on the job, having served previously as chief deputy coroner alongside his father, Warren W. Wood, before winning the election for county coroner in November 1959. Wood was tall and lean, wearing black-rimmed glasses that made him instantly recognizable as he stepped into the backyard. On his arrival, Wood was briefed on scene by the detectives. As Coroner Wood inspected the body,

East Eighth Street looking west. *Author's collection.*

Chimenti grouped with the detectives, motioning to the narrow entrance that led into the backyard.

"Creeping up from behind after she passed, the man must have put a crushing arm-lock about her throat." Chimenti gestured toward the ground. "While dragging her back through the narrow passageway between the two buildings, he may have slipped and fallen with her. Or, it could have been there that he assaulted her, before lugging the body back into the rear yard where it might remain undiscovered until daylight."

Laura Mutch. *Courtesy of the Kocher family.*

Chimenti's mental reenactment was interrupted by Coroner Wood as he informed detectives that he estimated the woman was murdered at least ten hours earlier, and the primary cause of death looked like strangulation. Wood also hinted at additional evidence that the woman had possibly been raped. Wood ordered the body removed to Hamot Hospital for the autopsy and excused himself as Chimenti and his men continued to theorize about the crime scene.

It was the whining of sirens that had attracted the attention of George Meucci and his brother-in-law as they stood outside 615 Holland Street that morning. As they approached the scene, Meucci overheard that a body had been found in the backyard. Approaching one of the nearby patrolmen, Meucci mentioned his mother had been reported missing earlier that morning and inquired as to the description of the body. Recognizing Meucci, officers placed him and his brother-in-law in the back seat of a police cruiser parked across the street by the No. 2 Jones Elementary School.

As the body was being removed from the rear of 717 Holland Street, the cruiser was maneuvered into the driveway in front of Konzel's garage. Meucci and his brother-in-law exited the car and were shown the body. Meucci confirmed that the body was that of his mother, Laura Mutch.

After the body was removed, detectives spotted that the ground underneath it had melted, most likely due to the victim's body heat at the time of death. Captain Chimenti and Sergeant Kalinowski set off for the Mutch residence while Detective Lupo entered the bottom duplex of Charlotte Clugh. Detective Malinowski, meanwhile, spoke with Peter Opalensky, the upstairs tenant of 717 Holland Street.

Inside Clugh's duplex, Lupo noticed Clugh's two German police dogs. Clugh nervously tousled her hair while retelling the events of the previous night, explaining that around ten o'clock, she was listening a new record on her hi-fi, Tennessee Ernie's hymns. In the front room, three children belonging to the Opalensky family and Clugh's own children were watching an episode of *The Twilight Zone*. Clugh remembered the time because ten o'clock was when show came on the television.

Around that time, Clugh told Lupo, she heard a whining noise that caught her attention; she believed the sounds were coming from her dogs. Clugh shrugged this off when she noticed her dogs in the front of the duplex, and she then went back to ironing her clothes. According to Clugh, she had recently acquired the dogs for protection, due to the increased attacks and burglaries in the neighborhood.

"We've had prowlers around here twice during the last month," Clugh continued. "Both times, I phoned the police after my dogs alerted me. But the prowlers got away before the officers arrived."

Clugh kept the dogs chained outside during the daytime and inside at night. Clugh told Lupo the dogs never caused trouble and only created a disturbance when they heard someone walking through the passageway into the rear of the yard, something they did not do the previous night. The only other information Clugh could provide was that she'd been outside around nine o'clock in the evening to remove clothes from the clothesline. She reported noticing nothing out of the ordinary then.

At the Mutch home, Chimenti and Malinowski confirmed the news to Laura's husband, George Meucci Sr., and spoke with him and several of the Mutch children, trying to find out some further information.

"Didn't your wife realize the danger of being alone on the streets in this neighborhood?" Chimenti asked. "Didn't you know about all the purse-snatching that's been going on, and the attempted assault on another housewife only a few nights ago?"

Meucci shrugged, explaining that they had just moved from Lawrence Park three weeks before and were unfamiliar with the neighborhood. This, coupled with the family's grief over burying their son, overshadowed any awareness of present danger in the area.

In Chimenti's mind, the murder raised a red flag, and he couldn't help but wonder if the attack from several days prior was in any way related to the murder of Laura Mutch. It was shortly before midnight on December 26 when a fifty-year-old woman arrived at headquarters, reporting she had been attacked. Speaking to police, she recalled her frightening ordeal.

"I was walking on 7th Street, between French and Holland, when a man who had been hiding in the shadows near my home leaped out at me," the woman told police between sobs. "He grabbed me from behind and kept one hand over my mouth so that I couldn't scream for help. Then he tried to drag me back into the alley behind a house. But I broke loose and ran."

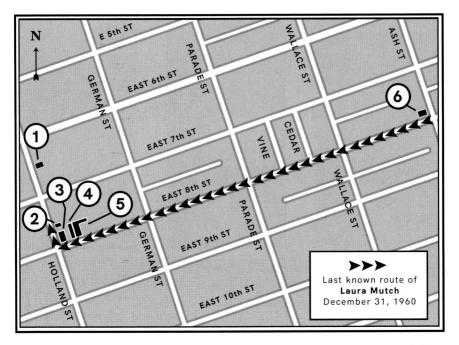

(1) The Mutch home, (2) 717 Holland Street, (3) Muffler King building, (4) Hill Mill Dairy, (5) Scobell Manufacturing and (6) Gospel Tabernacle Church.

The street where the woman was attacked was unlit, and despite there being no moon, she was able to provide a fairly good description of her attacker: a short, stocky white male dressed in dark slacks and a shirt, between thirty and forty years of age. He was unshaven and had bulging, dark eyes. Chimenti's mind replayed the woman's words over and over. What troubled him more was the suspect who had later been arrested and questioned in the attack. An investigation into his alibi checked out, and he was released within twenty-four hours. He couldn't have done it.

Or could he?

There were also the other attacks that had occurred since September. Late on the night of September 11, a seventy-five-year-old woman was returning home from a friend's house when she was grabbed from behind and dragged between two houses near 713 Holland Street by an unknown attacker, who then stole her purse, containing four dollars, before fleeing the area.

On December 28, 1960, around ten o'clock at night, another woman reported being followed by a white male in his twenties near French and Holland Streets. The man grabbed her, attempting to drag her off the

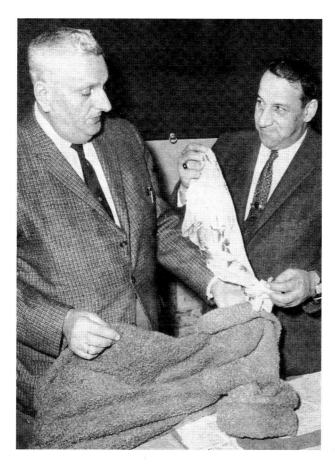

Detectives Carl
Malinowski and Philip
Lupo inspect Laura
Mutch's clothing.
Author's collection.

street into a nearby yard while trying to kiss her on the cheek. The woman screamed and fought her attacker, who then ran off.

And then there was December 30, 1960, around nine o'clock, just hours before Laura Mutch's murder, when another woman reported to police that she was seized from behind by a young man on East Seventh Street between Holland and German Streets. The woman's attacker stole her purse and ran south through a nearby alley, only five hundred feet from where Laura Mutch's body was found.

Coroner Wood, with the assistance of pathologist Dr. John A. Fust, began the examination of the body of Laura Mutch just after eleven o'clock in the morning, first examining, photographing and removing the scarf found wrapped around her mouth and throat. The scarf and the rest of the woman's clothing were placed into evidence bags and later turned over to Sergeant Kalinowski.

By eleven thirty, Dr. Fust had begun his external examination of the body. Fust documented the injures, which included:

> *marks in the skin,* [and] *the skin of the nose, her cheek bones and the cheeks and of the upper lip and of the chin showed linear markings. These consisted of red, slightly depressed parallel lines, about a sixteenth of an inch apart, and certainly representing impressions or abrasions due to firm contact with clothing having this configuration; there was a one inch band-like depression in the skin of the anterior surface of the neck above the Adam's apple. This was taken to have been caused by pressure of the scarf, which was said to have been tightly looped around the neck when the body was found.*

Additional injuries included:

> *The skin above the nipple on the right breast was slightly discolored, it was a faint bluish-purple; there was a half inch laceration of the skin of the left knee and two abrasions of the skin of the left knee on the side. I also found that the skin of the perineum, that is near her private parts, had been moistened slightly by watery pink fluid.*

An examination of the fluid found on the body later confirmed sperm was present. This, according to Dr. Fust, indicated Mutch had either recently had intercourse or been forcibly raped by her murderer. An internal examination of the organs indicated no signs of any preexisting conditions that would have caused or contributed to her death. There was a small hemorrhage noticed in the serous coverings of Mutch's heart, along with dark, unclotted blood in the heart, a common indication of asphyxia due to suffocation or strangulation.

Discussing the findings with Coroner Wood, Dr. Fust determined the cause of death was asphyxia, caused by Mutch's scarf being wrapped tightly around her neck. The pressure of the murderer's hands on both her mouth and nose then cut off her air supply, resulting in her death. Dr. Fust believed death could have been inflicted by someone with at least average strength and, despite early news reports indicating blood present at the scene, confirmed no evidence of external bleeding.

Captain Chimenti commented to reporters that several clues were located at the scene but declined to elaborate. The truth, however, was that detectives had very little physical evidence. Detectives Malinowski and Lupo, assisted by others within the detective bureau, were able to identify two suspects, who were arrested and taken into custody.

The first suspect, a fifty-two-year-old male, possessed a prior record of committing sex offenses against women and had served time in prison for these offenses. He had been out of prison for several months when he was picked up by detectives. The suspect was also a distant relative of Laura Mutch and lived close to the scene of the murder. He was booked without charges pending and grilled relentlessly by detectives. The suspect, however, denied all knowledge of or involvement in Laura Mutch's murder.

The second suspect, a twenty-four-year-old, had been arrested in Silver Creek, New York, after running out of gas and stealing an automobile on December 29. Charged with theft, this suspect was ordered held for a lie detector test to be scheduled in connection with the Mutch murder investigation.

Detectives Malinowski and Lupo filtered through the alibis of both men with a fine-tooth comb while Captain Chimenti reminded reporters that the men were presumed innocent until the investigation was completed. Conferring with District Attorney Herbert Johnson Jr. and the state police, assistance was requested by Chimenti in bringing a polygraph machine to Erie as soon as possible. Until then, the suspects would be held for ten days. During that time, detectives continued to check criminal files, focusing on those with known sex records. These sexual deviants, according to Chimenti, were interrogated but not held.

Later that night, just before midnight, a girl burst into a local café near Holland Street. "Call the police!" she screamed. "Another woman is being kidnapped!"

Within minutes, police arrived at the corner of Ash and East Tenth Streets to find a small crowd surrounding two women. One of them, a thirty-five-year-old woman, had been the victim of the apparent abduction.

"I was walking north on Ash when I approached a red convertible that was parked at the curb with a man on the passenger side of the front seat," the woman told officers. "As I came up even with the car, he opened the door, reached out and dragged me into the seat with him. I yelled, 'Let go! Let me go!' Just then, this girl came past and saw what was happening. She turned and ran back toward the café, screaming for help. The man let me go and got back behind the wheel of his car and sped off."

Two witnesses described the red convertible as a 1959 or 1960 Pontiac, with the numbers 850 or 580 on the black-and-white license plate.

Police set up roadblocks on all highways leading south, east and west out of the city, while an all-points bulletin was sent to local law enforcement in the area as well as New York and Ohio. Captain Chimenti worked on dispatching telegrams to motor vehicle departments in at least six states, along with a province in Canada, about the vehicle, attempting to track down the owners of any red 1959 and 1960 Pontiac convertibles.

As the investigation continued into the next day, the physical evidence recovered at the scene was sent to state laboratories in Harrisburg, as well as to the FBI in Washington, D.C. With detective teams working around the clock, they also continued piecing together Laura Mutch's last moments.

On the morning of January 2, 1961, Captain Chimenti held a briefing before reporters. Laura Mutch, Captain Chimenti stated, was believed to have been attacked from behind and grabbed around the face. The attacker's coat sleeve had possibly caused some scrapings on her face, but there were no signs of her having been beaten or bruised. "After she was gagged and throttled with her own head kerchief, [she was] then dragged around the north side of the house," Chimenti continued, "dropping her glasses and a Bible in the scuffle, and assaulted by the rear entrance to the residence of Mrs. Charlotte Clugh."

The two suspects still in custody, Chimenti added, were unable to corroborate either of their alibis. Both did readily volunteer to take a lie detector test. Despite reiterating that the men were innocent until proven guilty, Chimenti admitted he was "disturbed at discrepancies in their respective stories."

Investigating Laura Mutch's last moments, detectives confirmed she left the Gospel Tabernacle Church around ten o'clock and again declined numerous attempts by others to persuade her to accept a ride home. Although the investigation was spearheaded by Detectives Malinowski and Lupo, Captain Chimenti commented positively that the entire detective bureau had stepped up all efforts to find Mutch's murderer.

When asked about the types of offenders being brought in, Chimenti added that the Holland neighborhood between Seventh and Eighth, teeming with vagrants, winos and ex-cons, had been "cleaned-up" by detectives in their fervent search for Laura Mutch's killer. That night, additional suspects were picked up, including an Erie man who had grabbed and threatened a young waitress with a knife near Fourth and Peach Streets. The waitress was attacked on her way to work and reported the assault to police after her attacker was frightened off by several persons nearby. Later identified by witnesses, the attacker was picked up and brought into the station for questioning.

Lieutenant William Nevin of the state police shows results from polygraph examinations to Detective Chimenti while Detectives Lupo and Malinowski look on. *Erie Morning News.*

Captain Chimenti was later summoned and questioned the suspect, the fifth held in the investigation.

Around eight o'clock that night, Lieutenant William Nevin of the Pennsylvania State Police arrived from Harrisburg and began administering polygraph tests in the presence of Captain Chimenti and District Attorney Johnson. Late into the night, four of the suspects were cleared of any involvement in the murder. The results from the remaining two suspects appeared inconclusive, and they were charged, respectively, with assault and auto larceny charges unrelated to the murder.

Meanwhile, detectives began to look into Laura Mutch's life for any clues.

Laura Mutch was born on August 14, 1900, in the Borough of Volant, Pennsylvania, to fireman George Powell and Clarissa Snipe. By 1910, the

Powell family had moved from Volant to Washington Township in Erie County. At the age of seventeen, while residing in Wesleyville, Laura married thirty-two-year-old Leonard Meucci, an Italian immigrant who also used the surname Mutch, in Erie, Pennsylvania, on September 1, 1917. The marriage produced eight children, four boys and four girls, and at the time of Laura's death, she was survived by eighteen grandchildren. Following World War II, her husband, Leonard, became employed with Uniflow Manufacturing as a laborer, while Laura tended to the household.

A devoted housewife and mother to her eight children, Laura is still remembered fondly by surviving family members. A devout follower of religion, Laura found comfort in her Bible and attending prayer services. In December 1960, Laura and George's thirty-one-year-old son, Leonard, disappeared from their Wesleyville home and was later found dead from exposure. Grief-stricken, Laura found solace and healing in the words of scripture.

Friends and family arrived at A. Brugger & Sons Funeral Home on East Ninth Street on January 2 to pay their respects to Laura. Services were held the following day, January 3, 1961, at the funeral home, with her interment at Lakeside Cemetery. Families and friends huddled together in the bitter afternoon air as a Reverend Gibbons spoke before Laura's grave. Nearby, detectives from the Erie City Police Department kept a watchful eye in the hopes that her killer was among them.

At headquarters, Sergeant Kalinowski filtered through clothing taken from suspects brought in for questioning, comparing hair and fibers to those found on the clothing on Laura Mutch. Kalinowski painstakingly tried to find any evidence that would confirm Laura's killer came into physical contact with her prior to her death.

With Coroner Wood announcing the possibility of an inquest, and realizing they were not producing the results they hoped would lead to the killer, Captain Chimenti presented twelve detectives from the day shift orders to reexamine every possible clue. "The round-the-clock probe will continue until the police department has exhausted every possible clue and lead," Chimenti said to reporters.

This included a reenactment of Laura Mutch's final moments, including what was believed to be the route she traveled home prior to her death, which was done in the hopes of triggering additional leads. The reenactment included an elderly neighborhood woman dressed in similar clothes being shadowed by detectives and reporters. Reporters also observed, firsthand, the bizarre method by which Laura Mutch was strangled with her scarf, with

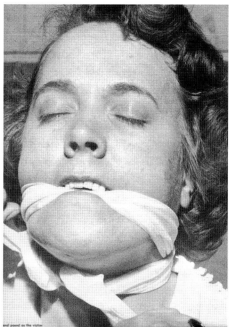

Left: A neighbor woman, dressed similarly to Laura Mutch, reconstructs her last moments in front of 717 Holland Street. *Erie Morning News*.

Right: Policewoman Lillian Strand demonstrates how Laura Mutch's scarf was tied around her mouth and neck. *Author's collection*.

Policewoman Lillian Strand being used to display the way in which the scarf was found tied around Laura's mouth.

Anonymous phone calls deluged the local switchboard, creating intense pressure on detectives to find the killer.

On January 5, Detective Sergeants Carl Englert and Nick Buto worked on several leads as the hunt intensified, with Detectives Wizikowski and Lapenz providing assistance. Although Captain Chimenti and his men would not comment on recent developments in the case, it materialized that the information focused on a twenty-year-old local man, described as a "beatnik," whom detectives claimed was responsible for attacks on women prior to Mutch's murder.

There was also a growing concern among detectives that there may be more than one criminal prowling the neighborhoods of Erie. As police cleared a sixth suspect on January 6, 1961, the *Erie Daily Times* declared that the search for Erie's Backyard Strangler had grown to be one of the greatest in the city's history, and as the investigation proceeded into its sixth day, Chief Edward

Present-day view of where 717 Holland Street once stood. *Author's collection.*

Williams remained confident the case would be solved. "We are continuing an around the clock probe," Chief Williams reassured the public.

Theories were continuing to metastasize by January 7, as detectives hoped desperately for the break needed to split the case wide open. Only a few details, however, remained confirmed: Laura Mutch had been walking home and was dragged off the street by an unknown individual who strangled and sexually assaulted her behind 717 Holland Street. Detectives theorized the killer could be a resident of the city or possibly a transient passing through. Others focused on the attacks prior to the murder, hoping that if a suspect was arrested in one of those cases, they could be tied to the Mutch murder.

A frantic Charlotte Clugh called police on the morning of January 8, believing a prowler was in her basement. Police raced to the scene, and a quick inspection revealed nothing to indicate anyone had attempted to break into the home. Clugh would vacate 717 Holland Street shortly thereafter in fear.

With over one hundred persons questioned and still no clear answers about the individual responsible for the murder, the investigation moved into the county, with Captain Chimenti ordering detectives to "spread out." Now assisting the investigation was the office of the district attorney,

Above: Present-day view of the backyard of 717 Holland Street, where Laura Mutch's body was found. *Author's collection.*

Right: County detective Roy Mong. *Author's collection.*

Grave of Laura Mutch, Lakeside Cemetery. *Author's collection.*

which included then–chief detective Roy Mong, a veteran of the Erie City Police Department. Mong assisted detectives by going through the records of known sexual deviants, female "scrapbooks" and other materials seized from past offenders.

Venturing back into the neighborhood of Holland and East Eighth Streets to question nearby residents, detectives were consistently faced with more dead ends. By then, police had heavily investigated every sexual deviant, sex offender and those with similar criminal histories known to them, only to come up empty-handed.

A frustrated Captain Chimenti spoke with reporters. "Someone living in that neighborhood knows more than he's saying," Chimenti said. "Those living in the immediate vicinity of the murder have given us practically no information. Any information, no matter how distant it may seem to be from the murder, could prove to be of extreme importance. There'll be no let-up in our investigation. The longer the killer evades us, the heavier we'll press."

Despite Captain Chimenti's declaration, others were less optimistic. "It looks now as though it will take a lucky break to help us solve one of the most wanton murders in the city's history," a veteran detective remarked to a reporter for the *Erie Daily Times.*

CHAPTER 2

FEAR CITY

I n his report for 1960, Erie County coroner Merle E. Wood reported six murders in Erie that year, with just one, the murder of Laura Mutch, remaining unsolved. This eclipsed both 1949 and 1956, in which Erie County had five murders each. And the way the investigation was shaping up, the Laura Mutch case appeared as if it would remain forever unsolved.

As the investigation progressed, detectives continued their search for Laura Mutch's purse, despite conflicting accounts from her family about whether she had one the night she was murdered. Detectives believed she was indeed carrying a purse and that the attack on her was related to the recent assaults and purse snatchings in the area. Despite another thorough search of the neighborhood, they once again were unable to locate anything of value.

Ten days into the investigation, without any viable suspects or leads, Erie had been thrown into pandemonium as police received a surge of frightened calls from people worried about nightly prowlers. Doors and windows were locked. Husbands kept tabs on their wives, making sure they were not alone after dark. Once the sun vanished, the darkness crept into the shadows of the twinkling city, with fear invading the homes of thousands of families.

"Don't even go to the corner store unless you have an escort," warned resident Doris Higby, when questioned by *Erie Daily Times* reporter Liz Becker. "I'm not taking any chances since this awful murder. I won't even answer the door until I'm absolutely sure who is outside."

State Street, downtown Erie, in 1958. *Erie County Historical Society.*

"Always double-check the locks before you go to bed," Higby concluded.

Higby's comments were echoed by thousands of women, who were equally frightened. "Stay home at night where you're safe. If you must go out be sure you're in a group," warned Elsie Stazer. "What's this city coming to? Things are getting worse every year."

On January 11, 1961, the FBI announced that it would become involved in the investigation once police established a prime suspect and a warrant was obtained, adding that the FBI could obtain a warrant charging the suspect with unlawful flight to escape persecution—presuming, of course, that the suspect had fled across state lines. The FBI's announcement was welcomed by Captain Chimenti.

Erie County commissioners, along with John Schiller, the administrator for Mayor Arthur J. Gardner, were approached by police in an effort to offer a $500 reward for information that would lead to the arrest and prosecution of Laura Mutch's murderer. This effort was also spearheaded by detectives who believed that the killer was local to the area, echoing Captain Chimenti's belief that someone was withholding information.

The Erie Magistrates Association also supported a reward, accepting a request by city police made during a luncheon on January 11 at the Elks Club, to furnish any information that might assist police with the murder.

These developments, of course, were not by any means an indication that the investigation had stalled, according to Captain Chimenti: "We are continuing to investigate every possible clue no matter how insignificant it may seem."

Talk of the reward solidified on January 13, when the Erie County commissioners approved the $500 reward.

With the addition of a reward, detectives slogged through suspect after suspect. Detective Inspector Frank Figaski, having returned to duty, questioned a prior suspect, a "known girl molester," after he was found drunk in his car near East Seventh and Holland Streets. The suspect, one of the first cleared by the state police's polygraph examination, continued to deny knowledge of the murder. An additional suspect, also arrested that night, was taken into custody near East Eighteenth and State Streets after boasting about the murder. Once he was brought in for questioning, police quickly learned he was intoxicated and knew nothing. The drunken suspect was booked without charge.

Captain Chimenti and Detective Sergeant Carl Kalinowski traveled to Washington, D.C., to personally deliver physical exhibits for laboratory tests in connection with the murder investigation and, as soon as they returned to Erie, rejoined the stagnant hunt for Laura Mutch's killer.

On the night of January 18, 1961, a woman driving around Perry Square, traveling to Erie's west side, observed a man following her in a tan station wagon. The station wagon followed her for several dozen blocks until she reached her home near West Third and Plum Streets. As she pulled into her driveway, the station wagon pulled up behind her vehicle. Frightened, the woman jumped from her vehicle, running to the nearby home of a neighbor to contact the police.

The station wagon peeled off into the night and disappeared.

Police soon responded and were provided with a description of the station wagon.

As January came to a close, Detective Inspector Figaski confirmed there were no recent updates. "We've uncovered nothing new here, but we're hoping for some good news from Washington later this week."

Captain Chimenti began to explore additional motives in the murder, suggested that maybe Laura Mutch was murdered to protect the killer's identity. "It could have been for that reason, or it could have been for a number of others," Chimenti said with a shrug. "Perhaps she knew the man well, or perhaps she never saw him before in her life. Right now we don't know, but we'll find out."

On Friday, January 27, 1961, Erie City Council increased the reward from $500 to $1,000, on the urging of Mayor Gardner and Police Chief Williams, with the city agreeing to contribute the additional $500 to the reward.

It was the January 15 murder of forty-one-year-old Margaret Urban, who was found raped and beaten to death in a car on Detroit's east side, that attracted the attention of Detective Inspector Figaski after he was notified by an Erie man who was in Detroit on business. Figaski probed authorities in Detroit about the murder and the suspect in custody, twenty-year-old Arnold Frasier, who was described as a transient.

Fraser confessed to the murder, telling police he and Urban left a bowling alley and drove around until Urban told Fraser she did not want to have anything to do with him. Fraser's alcohol-fueled temper escalated, and he beat Urban, raping her before strangling her. Figaski wanted to confirm whether Fraser could have been in or around Erie the night Laura Mutch was murdered. The probe ended when evidence proved Fraser was in Detroit on December 30, 1960.

On February 3, 1961, Detectives received the FBI's report on the examination of the physical evidence. Detective Figaski and the detectives studied the report and were surprised to learn that one of the items submitted for analysis, a jacket from one of the men arrested in the opening days of the murder, had bloodstains on it. Laura Mutch's distant relative, who had been excluded, was now viewed as the prime suspect.

The suspect, who resided in Pittsburgh, was confirmed to have been in Erie for several days before the murder and was known by police to have attended Laura Mutch's funeral. When questioned about why the suspect was released after the polygraph tests were administered, police indicated that the machines did not use the correct type of paper, rendering the results flawed and inconclusive.

Captain Chimenti arranged with the state parole department for the suspect to be brought to Erie for further questioning but instead traveled to Pittsburgh on February 21, after the state parole department scheduled an additional polygraph test. The interrogation, held at the Allegheny County Crime Laboratory, was accompanied by another polygraph test. The results, while indicating that the suspect was likely withholding information, showed no deception in his denial of Laura Mutch's murder.

A frustrated Chimenti, Malinowski and Lupo returned to Erie without an arrest and without answers.

The frustration had also spilled over among the citizens of Erie, ever so cognizant that Laura Mutch's murderer might never be caught.

"I'm writing you as a typical citizen, mother and housewife who had always admired women who would walk the streets alone at night—but not anymore," wrote one concerned Erie housewife under the pseudonym Stay-At-Homer. "In the meantime I suggest some of our Intelligent Detectives who are working around the clock (in offices) get to the seat of the problem by dressing up in women's clothes and walking in these areas where attacks often occur."

Others came to the defense of the police, including one individual who wrote a letter to the editor in response to the concerned housewife's editorial. "I strongly suggest that she stop playing policewoman and go back to playing housewife—where she belongs," the writer, identified only as "A Supporter," proclaimed. "Criticize when it is clearly justifiable; otherwise, get behind the wagon and push a little. I can plainly hear Stay-At-Homer howling with indignation when her husband criticizes her cooking."

As time wore on, the updates stopped. The fear, however, was not as easily forgettable.

On the night of February 28, 1961, twenty-year-old Betty Quick was walking home alone, having taken a shortcut through a field in the 2000 block of East Eleventh Street. Attacked by a man who attempted to grab her, Quick screamed and managed to break free, running to her home, located at 2040 East Seventh Street. Quick's husband left for the scene of the attack, attempting to locate his wife's attacker, but he was long gone. Quick's attacker was described as a tall white male. Police soon arrived and took Quick's statement, filing a report and cross-referencing the description with those of suspects already cleared in the Mutch investigation.

As the attacks continued, so did the carousel of colorful suspects.

Detective Sergeants Robert Ross and Mario Bagnoni responded to Fifth and State Streets after a tip was received about a possible suspect. The forty-year-old man was booked at the Erie City jail on an open charge, and his movements were checked by detectives. Another suspect, described as a middle-aged man, was picked up on April 26 by Detectives Malinowski and Lupo and hauled in for further questioning. The interrogation ended just as hundreds of others had before, with the individual released and no charges filed.

The $1,000 reward remained as thousands of gaunt tree limbs blossomed with the warmer weather, a sign that the cold, bitter night of December 31, 1960, was also fading from the public memory. On May 23, 1961, four more individuals were picked up by Captain Chimenti and Detectives Malinowski and Lupo and questioned at the Allegheny Crime Laboratory in Pittsburgh. Polygraph examinations were performed, and all persons were released.

As time wore on, members of the detective bureau were gradually reassigned from the Mutch investigation. Detectives Malinowski and Lupo remained in charge; however, they were slowly devoting more and more time to other cases. Updates on the case evaporated from the *Erie Daily Times* and *Erie Morning News*. And as May drifted into June, the nights became longer and warmer. Mothers were drawn to Perry Square, keeping an eye on their children as they danced around the public fountain, trying to beat the heat. Erie also was preparing for the tourist season that came with the warmer weather.

Amid sunsets on Presque Isle and attractions at nearby Waldameer, Erie's local amusement park, the reminder of the brutal attacks on women in Erie were nearly forgotten. For the terrified housewives in Erie, however, fear and terror would return again.

And soon.

CHAPTER 3

A MANIAC IN OUR MIDST

On June 2, 1961, seventy-two-year-old Clara Carrig was sitting in the living room of her first-floor apartment at 621 East Sixth Street, enjoying an uneventful morning with her ninety-three-year-old mother, Anna Clifton. It was just before nine forty-five when the doorbell sounded at the front door.

Clara entered the hallway, closing the door behind her before making her way to the front door. There, she was met by a man who informed her he was responding to the advertisement for the second-floor apartment currently available for rent. Clara stepped aside as the man entered. As was customary when her landlord was absent, Clara grabbed the key for the apartment, and they both proceeded to the second floor, with Clara leading the way.

On reaching the second floor and entering one of the bedrooms, empty save for a plain double bed, the man suddenly attacked Clara, throwing her to the ground, his hand clutching her throat. Her attempted screams were muffled by the iron grip fastened across her mouth.

The man leaned down, close to her ear.

"If you holler, I'll stab you!" he warned sternly.

The man's warning was followed by several blows, which rendered Clara unconscious.

Clara awoke several minutes later, lying half-naked across the bed, with one of her brown nylon stockings hanging around her bruised throat.

Clara stumbled to her feet, her words barely audible. Feeling a sharp pain in the pit of her stomach, she clutched her abdomen. She pulled her hands away, stained with blood. Falling to her knees as she entered the hallway, Clara let out a gut-wrenching scream.

"Somebody stabbed me!" she sobbed.

Clara's husband, Thomas, rushed up the stairs and assisted Clara to her feet. Together, they hobbled carefully down the stairs to the first-floor landing before Thomas ran to a nearby neighbor's home and called the fire department. At 10:04 a.m., howling sirens pierced the air as firemen from the local inhalator squad arrived on scene.

Firemen entered the front door, finding Clara wrapped in a blanket saturated with blood.

Around 10:15 a.m., police converged on the home; Detective Sergeants Robert Ross and Maurice Sheehan were the first investigators to arrive on scene. Sergeant Sam Gemelli searched the second floor, gun drawn, and discovered a rear door leading to the back hall of the home, which led outside—the likely escape route of Clara's attacker.

An ambulance raced Clara to Hamot Hospital. Detectives Ross and Sheehan questioned Thomas Carrig and his mother-in-law, learning nobody besides Clara had seen her attacker. Patrolmen and detectives fanned out

Present-day photograph of 621 East Sixth Street. *Author's collection.*

to neighboring homes to see if anyone had witnessed someone fleeing the Carrig home.

Upon her arrival at Hamot Hospital, Clara was sedated and rushed into surgery as doctors tried to save her life. Her abdomen had been punctured by a sharp knife or blade, going through her kidney and almost exiting out of her back. Additional injuries indicated she had been struck by a fist or by a blunt instrument, and there was evidence of sexual assault.

As Clara was in surgery, a tri-state alert and all-points bulletin were sent to local law enforcement agencies. At the Carrig apartment, Detective Kalinowski studied the crime scene for fingerprints and collected evidence. At Hamot Hospital, doctors advised detectives that the weapon used to stab Clara was most likely a long blade, possibly a military-style bayonet, providing a clue that sent detectives rushing to surplus stores and making inquiries with local military reserve units to check for any stray or missing bayonets.

From the beginning, detectives noticed similarities between the attack on Clara Carrig and the murder of Laura Mutch. Both victims were elderly and had been throttled or strangled and sexually assaulted.

Following her surgery, Clara was heavily sedated and on oxygen. Her husband, Thomas, kept a lonely vigil at her bedside. Clara had lost a lot of blood and had one of her kidneys removed. Despite the odds, doctors were able to save her life.

Bill Rogosky of the *Erie Morning News* interviewed Thomas Carrig outside of Clara's hospital room. "I can't understand why anyone would want to pick on us," Thomas said, baffled. "Clara and I are both up in age."

Thomas told Rogosky what happened that morning, admitting ashamedly that when Clara was attacked, he was in the bedroom, making the bed and cleaning up. Thomas Carrig said it was about ten or fifteen minutes after hearing the doorbell that he heard "one of the most awful screams" he ever heard in his life and rushed upstairs, where he found his wife bleeding profusely.

"She was standing slumped in the hallway with her arms tightened around her abdomen. Her assailant apparently escaped through the back way," Thomas said, shaking his head in disbelief. "Clara is a wonderful woman. Neither of us has ever harmed anyone in our life."

Following their tenure running the old Bodega Restaurant, Clara and Thomas were now in retirement and wanted to take it easy for the rest of their lives.

Thomas started to return to his wife's room before looking back to Rogosky. "I'm going to have to go out tomorrow and see if I can get some

Thomas Carrig speaks to reporter Bill Rogosky. Clara Carrig is shown in insert. *Erie Morning News*.

blood donors. They used a lot to save Clara's life, and I want to replace it in the blood blank."

Captain Chimenti was convinced that both Clara Carrig and Laura Mutch were attacked by a mental deviant, possibly the same individual. "We've never had a case like this new one," Chimenti said. "But you never can tell just how a mad man is going to operate."

Later that night, Clara regained consciousness, enough to be interviewed by the detectives who also kept an around-the-clock vigil at her bedside. Detectives Mike Snider and Simon Demchak questioned Clara about the attack, trying to confirm a description of her attacker. Clara remembered him as being a thin white male between twenty and thirty years of age wearing a blue shirt, with dark hair and a sallow complexion. She had never seen the man before.

"When we had gone upstairs to look at the apartment, he knocked me to the floor and held me down," Carrig sheepishly told Detective Snider. "He told me not to make any noise, but I screamed. Then he stabbed me."

In response to the attack, Chief Edward Williams devoted all available resources and manpower to the area around Clara's home. Officers and detectives continued going door to door, questioning anyone they came across about what they witnessed that morning.

Clara remained hospitalized in critical condition the following day, although doctors believed that her chances of recovery were positive. Detectives knew that they were fortunate to have a victim who had lived to tell the tale and seized upon this opportunity to find her attacker. Captain Chimenti collected a series of mug shots, prepared for Clara when she was in an improved condition, in an attempt to identify her attacker.

"We're not letting up for a minute. Every available man is handling some part of this investigation," Chimenti told reporters.

In the days that followed, detectives returned to 621 East Sixth Street and painstakingly examined the area behind the house, attempting to locate evidence that could have come from Clara's attacker when he fled from the rear of the home. Detective Sergeants Wizikowski and Lapenz visited Clara in the hospital to obtain additional information from her but were unsuccessful because of her weakened state. Digging into Clara's past, detectives also looked into the possibility of the attack being related to a prior incident in which she witnessed a robbery at the Lake City Finance Company building in 1954. Later that year, twenty-seven-year-old Gregory Beery of Girard confessed to four counts of armed robbery and was convicted of the crime. Police came to the conclusion there was likely no connection.

Attempts to trace the weapon used proved difficult, and with additional questioning came inconsistent statements from Clara regarding the description of her attacker. Despite the impasse, detectives were hopeful, acknowledging that it was understandable why eyewitness descriptions from victims such as Clara could be inconsistent.

As far as suspects, police arrested a recently released convict who admitted to having been apartment hunting around East Sixth Street at the time of the attack. After two hours of questioning, police were satisfied with his alibi, and he was released from custody. An additional suspect, a Millcreek Township resident with a record of criminal assaults, was arrested on June 5 and taken to Hamot Hospital, where he was presented before Clara, who had just been downgraded from critical condition. The man, Clara told detectives, was not her attacker.

As Clara's condition improved, Detective Inspector Figaski presented numerous mug shots of repeat offenders to her. Clara labored over the photographs, studying them intently, but was only able to partially identify men with similar build, hair and facial structure, making a positive identification difficult. Over time, as her condition improved, police furiously attempted to locate her attacker, all while collecting files and mug shots for Clara to review once her condition improved. "We are hopeful she will be able to identify her unknown assailant," Figaski told reporters.

While detectives hoped a living victim would provide the break they needed to arrest the person responsible for the attack and possibly the murder of Laura Mutch, police had struck a dead end by June 8, with Captain Chimenti confirming they had no updates.

With no additional plans to question Clara or review mug shots until she had improved, detectives were once again faced with inconsistent details in another frightening crime. This presented relentless frustration for detectives, who, despite arresting suspects who were possibly responsible for the crime, ultimately saw them cleared by Clara herself as not being responsible.

Fear, however, continued to spread throughout Erie.

Erie Daily Times columnist Red Barr, writing for his column "BARR-B-Q" on June 11, 1961, declared a "madman was on the loose" in Erie. Barr's column quoted, anonymously, members of the police department who believed the person who attacked Clara Carrig was also responsible for Laura Mutch's murder. "A maniac may be in our midst," Barr wrote. "One who periodically strikes at elderly women, it is feared."

Barr, a native Clevelander, wrote that the attacks against women in Erie brought to mind the same terror that plagued Cleveland during the reign of the Mad Butcher of Kingsbury Run in the 1930s. The so-called torso murders, warned Barr, were never solved. Barr's column did little to calm the growing panic that had started to resurface, and police were once more inundated with phone calls from frightened housewives and young women afraid of prowlers who were refusing to leave their homes unattended.

While Clara remained hospitalized, she received hundreds of greeting cards, with many writing their thoughts and prayers for a speedy recovery. By June 14, police still had no solid leads and decided to wait until Carrig was fully recovered to present additional mug shots and a possible lineup of known offenders. Additional suspects were still taken to Hamot Hospital to be brought before Clara Carrig.

The responses were all the same: "He is innocent, you can let him go."

Investigators utilized the opportunity to question suspects about their potential involvement in the murder of Laura Mutch. Detective Inspector Figaski was adamant that despite a lack of apparent clues, his men would continue to hunt Carrig's attacker and bring him to justice, no matter the cost.

Warmer temperatures brought with them an inundation of crime, which included more burglary cases. Clara continued to steadily improve from her wounds, and on July 2, 1961, she was released from the hospital. Returning to her home with her husband, Clara would never forget the kindness shown by the hundreds of citizens who wrote to her.

"I wish to express my heartfelt thanks to everyone for their many prayers, masses, flowers, cards and other acts of kindness during my recent stay in the hospital," Carrig wrote in a response in the *Erie Daily Times*. She also made a special note for the nurses and doctors at Hamot, along with the blood donors who saved her life, and hoped that with the passage of time, she could put her horrible ordeal behind her.

CHAPTER 4

DUST AND ENIGMAS

J ust after 2:20 a.m. on July 5, 1961, Karl Malm, a resident of 425 Peach Street, spotted an individual setting drapes on fire in the hallway of the Lininger Apartments. Malm phoned police, who then notified the fire department. Around 2:36 a.m., an apartment home at 518 Sassafras Street was also set on fire.

Patrolman Ed Pianka, driving on his beat, spotted the fire at 518 Sassafras and reported it to the fire department. Several minutes later, a third call was placed to the police switchboard by an unidentified individual, reporting a fire at the Vernon Doyle Apartments at 302 West Sixth Street.

Around 3:00 a.m., Pianka arrived at West Sixth and Sassafras Streets, parked his cruiser and dimmed his headlights. He had just returned from one of the apartments that had caught fire that night. An arsonist was on the loose in Erie, and Pianka had been ordered to scout the area.

As Pianka scanned the streets, he spotted a young white male wearing a black jacket and striped shirt walking along West Sixth Street and determined that he did not match eyewitness accounts of the suspected arsonist. It was then that the man started to act suspiciously, disappearing from view and then reappearing moments later.

Feeling a hunch, Pianka decided to follow the man. Reaching the corner of West Fifth and Myrtle Streets, he stopped his cruiser.

"Hey, you!" Pianka called out.

Pianka heard something hit the ground and immediately spotted a knife that had fallen from the man's jacket. Pianka parked his cruiser and

Patrolman Ed Pianka. *Erie Daily Times.*

arrested the man on a knife-carrying charge. Within minutes, Pianka arrived downtown with the man, and he was identified as twenty-six-year-old Richard Worlund of 803 East Twenty-First Street.

As Worlund was being searched, officers found eight packs of matches, in addition to a dozen household matches. Pianka made the connection that Worlund was possibly linked to the fires and decided to retrace his steps. Near West Fifth and Myrtle Streets, Pianka found several letters addressed to 332 West Sixth Street. Police confirmed the letters were taken from one of the mailboxes of the buildings set on fire.

Detective Sergeants Malinowski and Lupo, assisted by Detectives Wizikowski and Lapenz, questioned Worlund during the early hours that morning. Worlund readily admitted to setting the three fires because he was rejected by a woman who lived at Fourth and State Streets. The rejection left him "mad at the world."

"All indications are that this guy would have gone on all night unless stopped," Deputy Fire Chief Jon North told reporters, praising the quick reaction by Erie's police and fire departments. "The Lord was with us."

The case against Richard Worlund was given an additional review by veteran detectives, who noticed similarities between Worlund's appearance and the description of Clara Carrig's attacker. Detectives looked harder into Worlund after he admitted to pulling a knife on a woman while she entered her car in downtown Erie the year before. The incident was never reported to police.

Piecing together Worlund's background suggested he possessed a tendency for violence. The fact that he also went on an arson spree after being rejected by a woman cemented him as a viable suspect.

District Attorney Johnson held a conference on the morning of July 6, 1961, with Detective Inspector Figaski. Both men discussed the arson case as well as its possible connection with the stabbing and assault of Clara Carrig. Johnson announced he would order a psychiatric examination of Worlund, preceding any lie detector examination.

Right: Arsonist Richard Worlund. *Erie Daily Times*.

Below: Erie's east side neighborhood as it appeared in the 1960s. *Erie County Historical Society*.

When asked about Laura Mutch and Clara Carrig, Worlund denied his involvement in either case. "I never harmed a woman in my life," Worlund told detectives. Police admitted they had nothing to link him to the crimes but decided to parade Worlund before Clara at her home prior to District Attorney Johnson's conference with police. Clara struggled to take herself back to those frightening moments.

"I don't think he's the one," Carrig told detectives Snider and Demchak. "I'm not sure. His hair is a little different."

Despite Worlund's denial in the Mutch and Carrig cases, police were not quick to exclude him as a suspect.

"His whole pattern of behavior, his physical description and the knife he was carrying when Patrolman Pianka arrested him makes him a prime suspect," Detective Inspector Figaski declared, pointing to evidence he believed proved that Worlund was a danger to women.

Worlund was "obviously obsessed with women or he couldn't have become so furious just because he couldn't make a date with a strange girl," according to Figaski.

Police were contacted by a woman who confirmed that Worlund stayed at her residence the night of December 30 and 31, 1960, to help her husband with their car. After an examination by doctors in Erie, Worlund was sent to Warren State Hospital for commitment along with additional psychiatric observations.

Erie moved on.

On July 22, 1961, the American Legion ended its state convention, which brought nearly ten thousand delegates to the city, concluding with a parade consisting of six thousand marchers and music from twenty colorful drum and bugle corps. Around two forty-five in the afternoon, nearly one hundred thousand men, women and children lined the parade route in sweltering eighty-four-degree temperatures. As the parade progressed, nearly three hundred marchers and pedestrians collapsed from the heat and required treatment.

On the morning of August 2, 1961, thunderstorms roared through the area, with lightning and a downpour of rain causing $1,000 in damages. The storm dredged up frightening memories of the infamous 1915 Millcreek flood, still remembered by Erieites. Mary Hafey, a twenty-six-year-old Erie schoolteacher, set off from Long Point, Canada, at four o'clock in the afternoon in her fourth attempt to cross Lake Erie, planning to finish in North East. Just after ten o'clock, nearly six miles in, both cold water and stomach cramps forced Hafey to abandon her effort to traverse Lake Erie.

That fall, 21,382 students in Erie returned to public schools as summer came to an end. Thirty-four-year-old Stephen Calafato went on trial for his role in the armed robbery at Eckerd's drugstore on Peach Street; he was found guilty after two hours of deliberation and faced a twenty-year term in addition to fines totaling $10,000.

On September 28, 1961, Detective Sergeants Carl Malinowski and Billy Shannon picked up a forty-year-old male and interrogated him for several hours. Although he was not held, detectives indicated that he may have provided information that could prove valuable in being able to trace the murderer.

"Investigators have been working in the dark mostly but I think there is a chance of breaking this case eventually," Malinowski reflected on the investigation, now in its ninth month.

"This case is far from being closed," declared Detective Inspector Figaski, defending the investigation.

Leads trickled in through the month of October, when police questioned two new suspects in relation to the murder of Linda McGee in Cleveland, Ohio. McGee had been stabbed behind her home by a prowler, according to Cleveland police. Although there were stark similarities between the McGee murder and the Mutch and Carrig cases, Captain Chimenti determined no likely connection between the two.

As quickly as the leads reappeared in the Mutch and Carrig cases, they once again dissipated.

That November, described as one of the driest seen in the past several years, things were changing downtown. This included the Erie Central Mall, located at Peach and Eighteenth Streets, opening with much enthusiasm. Over one hundred acres consisting of eight hundred thousand cubic yards of fill were approved for the East Bay Land Reclamation Project for Erie's bayfront, planned for future industrial development by 1962. Mayor Arthur Gardner hailed the announcement, calling it "the fitting together of yet another piece of the overall Erie renaissance program."

Gardner himself had also been focused on the mayoral campaign of 1961, which pitted him against Dr. Charles B. Williamson. Fifty thousand citizens were originally projected to vote on November 7, 1961, as the campaigns wrapped up in an exciting climax. Erieites awoke on the morning of November 8, 1961, to see Dr. Charles B. Williamson had pulled off a stunning upset, defeating Mayor Gardner. Although Gardner lost his reelection campaign, he would remain for two more years as a city councilman.

The one-year anniversary of Laura Mutch's death came and went without an arrest.

The following article appeared on page 13 of the December 29, 1961 edition of the *Erie Daily Times*:

> *One year ago tomorrow night Mrs. Laura Mutch was murdered. The following morning the 60-year-old woman's body was found in snow in back of a house near 7th and Holland. Strangulation had caused her death and the killer remains at large. A $1,000 reward still stands for the capture of the slayer. City Council and county commissioners each posted $500 of the reward. The little woman was on her way home from church services when she was grabbed by a fiend and dragged off the street and gagged.*

The anniversary was also met with silence from detectives as 1961 ended with heavy snowstorms, ice and bitter temperatures pummeling most of the country.

Dr. Charles B. Williamson took the oath of office as mayor on January 1, 1962, and prospects for Erie remained promising for the new year, especially with low unemployment and plentiful jobs. On January 5, 1962, an advertisement appeared in the *Erie Daily Times* seeking bids for dismantling and removing the old two-story duplex at 717 Holland Street, which would reduce and grade the location to ground level. By February 1962, the building was razed.

Cold temperatures disappeared in February, with warmer temperatures hitting fifty-nine degrees. Warmer temperatures resulted in a record 55,683 visitors coming to view the peninsula. The beginning of the year still saw some tragic car crashes as Erie was continually blanketed with heavy drifts of snow. Burglaries and muggings also continued to plague the police department, and numerous pinball violations—during a time when pinball machines were outlawed due to their possible effect on crime—attracted the attention of Mayor Williamson.

Williamson's next steps would create waves within local government, just several months into the beginning of his administration.

Rumors began circulating in March 1962 of an impending shakeup within the police department. The rumors, deemed credible by the *Erie Daily Times*, included changes from top to bottom within the department, starting with Captain George Radaker replacing Chief Edward Williams. Other personnel changes saw Detective Sergeant Chester Miller replace Frank Figaski as the inspector of detectives and Captain Chimenti move to inspector of patrol and traffic divisions, roles that would be combined in the new shift.

When pressed for further comment by the *Erie Daily Times*, Mayor Williamson claimed the report was unfounded. This was in stark contrast to leaks confirming the report, which occurred during a meeting in the office of Safety Director Richard Hetico.

The rumors were confirmed on March 27, 1962, when the widespread changes within the Erie City Police Department were announced. Not only were the rumors confirmed, but there were also other changes, such as the elimination of ten street corner patrolmen, officers who were fixed on street corners where they performed their duties. Now, these officers were assigned to regular beats in heavily traversed areas. Beats within State Street and adjoining areas were changed, with patrols in those areas projected to improve both traffic conditions and protection for pedestrians.

The changes also called for an expansion of officers engaging in foot traffic and motorcycle officers in busy areas with heavy vehicle and pedestrian activity. The juvenile division saw an expansion in manpower to include three patrolmen and a female clerk. Officer Lillian Strand was moved and provided with a temporary assignment in the division whenever needed.

Not all changes were viewed positively, and one of the casualties of the sweeping changes was Detective Inspector Figaski, who was demoted to the rank of patrol officer. Figaski, said to have had a longstanding personality clash with those now suddenly in charge, was not willing to give those superiors the opportunity of such a move, and he subsequently retired, weeks shy of twenty-five years of service with the Erie City Police Department.

Mayor Williamson's shakeup infuriated many in the police department, especially many who had supported his election. Soon, an organized protest was planned, with those who protested saying the changes ignored those who supported Williamson's candidacy for mayor and pointing out that Richard Hetico, Chief George Radaker and Deputy Chief Armand Chimenti were top officials within the department during Gardner's administration. Radaker and Hetico disagreed, defending the personnel moves as being based on merit alone and not politics.

Those who disagreed with the changes also pointed to the way Frank Figaski was treated, along with four other veteran officers forced to seek retirement, including former chief Edward Williams.

Following the hottest May since 1944, June was known as a banner month for the Most Reverend John Mark Gannon as he received an honorary degree celebrating his eighty-fifth birthday. Susan Peterman was crowned "Miss Erie," and the new widescreen film projection medium, Cinerama, opened with a benefit staged by Erepa Grotto.

Carl Malinowski set time aside on the morning of July 10, 1962, to paint the outside of his house. Around noon, as he climbed down from his ladder, Malinowski experienced chest pains and informed his wife, Mary, that he felt like he was having a heart attack. Malinowski was rushed to the emergency room at St. Vincent Hospital, where it was confirmed he had suffered a heart attack. A few hours after being admitted to the hospital, Malinowski suffered a myocardial rupture and died at seven o'clock in the evening at the age of fifty-nine.

His death caused a ripple effect throughout the entire police department. "I think we have lost an exemplary police officer, one who is an example for everybody to follow," Mayor Charles Williamson commented to the *Erie Daily Times*. "Though I did not know him well, I know of his work, and it left nothing to be desired. He's not replaceable."

Chief Radaker equally praised Detective Malinowski's work: "He was a good, clean living man, certainly a great asset to the department, and a big loss to the department."

By July 17, Chief Radaker announced appointments within the department following Malinowski's death. Lieutenant Carl Kalinowski was promoted to the rank of captain, Sergeant Donald Gunter was promoted to lieutenant of the bureau's identification and records office and Patrolman Edward Respecki was promoted to sergeant. The promotions, which took effect immediately, fell under the direction of Deputy Chief Chester Miller and Safety Director Hetico, who informed reporters that the three officers were "the best men for the jobs."

Several days later, police were again placed on high alert.

Another woman had been attacked.

CHAPTER 5

DOWNPOUR OF DEATH

It was 12:25 p.m. on July 20, 1962, when twenty-seven-year-old Helen Knost finished paying a bill at Halle's Department Store in the West Erie Plaza. The sunnier weather had disappeared, with threatening black clouds dumping sheets of rain. Helen regretted parking along a sidewall secluded from the main parking lot and bowed to fate as she made a mad dash for her car.

Reaching her car, Helen unlocked the door and dropped into the driver's seat. Just as she placed her key in the ignition, her passenger door was thrust open as a man climbed inside. Startled at what she could only describe later as a "fresh kid," her beginning protest was silenced when he pulled out a kitchen knife.

The man reached into his right pocket, producing rope that was looped on both ends. Placing one loop around Helen's right wrist, he was proceeding to tie the other around her left wrist when they both spotted a Millcreek police cruiser passing through the parking lot.

Helen lunged toward the horn, trying to alert the cruiser, and the man pressed the knife into her ribs, warning her. Helen froze as the police cruiser disappeared into the rainy haze. Her attacker then ordered her from the car, placing her into a vehicle that was parked next to hers, described as a grayish or light cream-colored Volkswagen.

Inside his car, the man finished looping Helen's wrists, tying them to the emergency brake handle in the center of the vehicle. As he started the car, the calm demeanor he had exhibited vanished, his hands shaking as he attempted to light a cigarette before discarding his pack into Helen's purse.

West Erie Plaza as it would have appeared in 1962. *Courtesy of John L. Scott Sr.*

As raindrops exploded against the windshield with increasing intensity, Helen's abductor drove behind the buildings of West Erie Plaza before turning left on West Eighth Street, heading westbound. Helen kept a careful eye on her abductor as they turned onto Powell Avenue before making another turn onto Route 5, continuing west as they entered Fairview.

At Eaton Road, Helen's abductor took a sharp right, heading toward the lake about three hundred yards before stopping.

As she started to become sick in the car, Helen's face was pummeled with blows from the man before he placed his hands around her neck, starting to choke her. Helen fought for air as she tried to wriggle her hands free from the taut rope.

"I can't breathe…" she gasped, her face trembling.

The man brought his face close to hers.

"I don't want you to breathe."

Helen struggled to scream before her attacker tore off one of her stockings, jamming it down her throat.

Then, she lost consciousness.

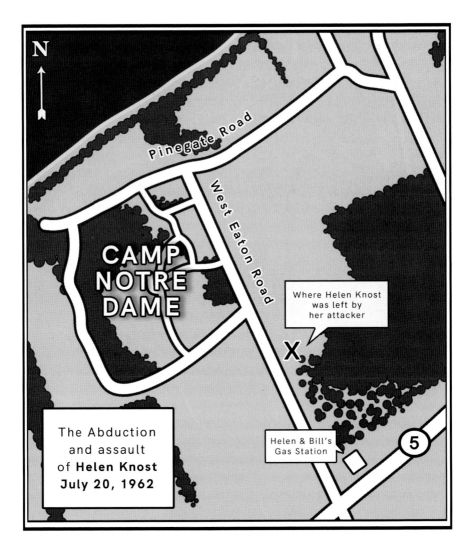

The Abduction and assault of **Helen Knost** July 20, 1962

Where Helen Knost was left by her attacker

Helen & Bill's Gas Station

Hours later, Helen's eyes fluttered open as the rain peppered her face. She gradually came to, finding that she had been discarded in a ditch alongside the road, covered with sticks and other foliage. The world around her was a blur as she clawed through the muddy earth toward the road, where she once against lost consciousness.

Drifting in and out consciousness, missing one of her shoes, Helen plodded south on Eaton Road until she reached Helen and Bill's gas station on the corner of Route 5. Stumbling inside, her dark slacks, black-and-gray checkered blouse and silk scarf muddied and saturated with blood, Helen collapsed to the floor.

Present-day view of Eaton Road, looking north, the area where Helen Knost was discarded by her attacker. *Author's collection.*

The Fairview Fire Department arrived on scene and discovered to their horror that her throat had been slashed.

Helen was rushed to Hamot Hospital, where doctors were able to stabilize her. Her injuries consisted of two deep gashes to her neck, from ear to ear, and severe lacerations to her forehead, with both eyes cut. Both of her wrists also exhibited signs of rope cuts and cuts made by her attacker.

Detective Tyco Lange of the Pennsylvania State Police was assigned to head the investigation. As Helen was recovering that night, police returned to Eaton Road for clues that could assist them. Detectives from both Erie and Millcreek provided additional assistance in an attempt to locate the attacker, whom the press described as a "homicidal maniac."

By the end of the night, investigators had been unable to find any evidence that could lead them to Helen's abductor. Her purse, which contained forty dollars in cash, was never found.

On July 23, 1962, a suspect was arrested by state police detectives and taken to Hamot Hospital, where he was paraded before Helen, who confirmed he was not her attacker. The suspect was promptly released.

Present-day intersection of Route 5 and Eaton Road, the former location of Helen and Bill's gas station. *Author's collection.*

Almost immediately, the viciousness of the attack drummed up talk of a possible connection to the Mutch and Carrig cases. These cases, in addition to fifteen others since September 1960, were dubbed by the *Erie Morning News* as Erie's "phantom attacker" cases.

Chester J. Miller, deputy chief of the Erie City Police Department, was not optimistic that Helen Knost's attack was related to the Carrig case. "There is nothing to indicate similarity to the Mutch case either," Miller claimed to reporters.

Under the direction of Detective Lange, police sifted through additional leads, and on July 25, 1962, Helen, along with Lange, spoke to *Erie Morning News* reporter Bill Campbell about her encounter.

Heavily bandaged and bruised, Helen strained to talk, still in disbelief about what occurred. "I know there are some people who don't believe this really happened to me. I still can't believe it myself, but look at me."

A description of Helen's attacker was also provided:

> *The suspect is described by police as about eighteen years old, with a thin and narrow face, having a blond crew-cut and wearing light colored trousers and a striped and long sleeved t-shirt.*

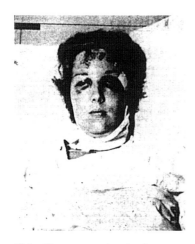

Helen Knost recovering the day following her attack. *Erie Morning News*.

The attack, recounted in the *Erie Morning News* and the *Erie Daily Times*, was met with skepticism from members of the public who did not accept Helen's story, which angered Detective Lange. "This is the McCoy," Lange said to those who questioning the validity of the attack. "I only wish that all the women in Erie would realize this. We have a psychopath roaming the streets and he could do this to someone else!"

Further leads in the investigation included a blonde twenty-year-old male, who owned a cream-colored Volkswagen similar to the one described by Helen. This lead, however, turned out not to be related to the attack.

Detective Lange remained positive. "We are checking everyone who fits the description Mrs. Knost has given us, and someday we'll catch up with him."

Almost a week after the attack, state police detectives found themselves in a similar position to that of the Erie City Police, with leads shrinking and the case growing colder by the minute.

Detective Lange decided to make an impassioned plea to the public for help. "For his own protection, as well as society's, this sick boy must be stopped before he strikes again," Lange declared before reporters. "The next time he may be a killer instead of an assaulter."

Not completely discounting a connection to other attacks in Erie, Detective Lange reminded the public of unsolved assault cases that followed a similar pattern. On July 28, 1962, authorities proposed a reward of $1,000 in hopes of "smoking out" Helen Knost's attacker, with county commissioners Louis Rzymek and Fred Lamberton declaring that the reward could be offered at the upcoming meeting. This was supported by Commissioner Carl Proctor and members of the Millcreek Police Department in pursuing the "probable psychopath."

County commissioner Lamberton also took the time to remind the public of the still-standing reward of $1,000 in the Laura Mutch case.

"Women in the community are frightened," remarked District Attorney Johnson, confirming that the fear stalking the city had leaked beyond it into the neighboring suburbs.

The investigation itself had spread as far as Franklin, Pennsylvania, when Venango County sheriff David Berenson became suspicious of an AWOL soldier from Niagara Falls, New York. Discovering a knife and a piece of rawhide in the soldier's belongings, and armed with a bulletin describing Knost's attacker, Berenson brought the eighteen-year-old soldier to Erie for questioning. He was cleared and returned to the Venango County Jail.

The day after the proposed reward was announced, Helen was released from the hospital.

County commissioners voted on July 31, 1962, to approve the $1,000 reward, viewed as a last ditch-effort, for any person who could provide information leading to the arrest and conviction of Helen's attacker.

Detective Sergeant Leo Weir of the Pennsylvania State Police had almost seen it all. The forty-six-year-old native of Duquesne had led an exciting life, playing semiprofessional football in 1936, working at Kennywood Amusement Park and grinding it out in the Duquesne steel mills and the Civilian Conservation Corps before entering the Pennsylvania State Police Academy in 1940.

With the outbreak of World War II and after being transferred to the state police barracks in Lawrence Park, Weir volunteered for the U.S. Navy and was assigned to a subchaser in the Pacific. Following the war, Weir returned to the state police, where he saw involvement in some of the most notorious cases in northwestern Pennsylvania.

Assisting with the Knost investigation, Weir conferred with investigators in Beaver County after learning about the arrest of a homicide suspect in a case that occurred in New Sewickley Township. The body of Doretta Dean Schultz had been found by a road, and a man named Carrol Williams was arrested in Crestline, Ohio, for her murder. After having a conference with the Beaver County investigators and after determining that Williams did not match the physical profile of Helen's attacker, Weir excluded him as a suspect.

On August 8, investigators met with Helen to produce a sketch of her attacker. The composite, drawn by William Rusterholtz of the *Erie Daily Times* with the assistance of a state police artist, was believed to be a valuable tool in locating Helen's attacker, according to Detective Sergeant Weir. "Mrs. Knost has a good picture in her mind of her assailant and can definitely identify him," said Weir to reporters when plans for the composite sketch were discussed.

Despite both the *Erie Daily Times* and *Erie Morning News* indicating that state police detectives had run out of leads, Weir disputed these reports. "We

Composite sketch of Helen Knost's abductor. *Erie Morning News.*

are working on a lot of leads and we still feel the assailant drives a light colored Volkswagen. His outstanding feature is hair that is almost white, more blond than usual."

By mid-August, Helen had been approached by police to identify at least nine suspects. These "lineups" failed to positively identify her attacker. Police also followed up on leads related to light- or cream-colored Volkswagens in the state, checking all persons who owned that type of vehicle by reaching out to dealers and sifting through car registration records.

One clue police released to the public was that, according to Helen, her attacker's Volkswagen had a unique red sticker on the windshield.

Detective Tyco Lang, after speaking with Helen and her husband, Richard, suggested they undergo lie detector tests. Both readily agreed without hesitation, and a review of the results indicated no deception by either Helen or her husband.

On Thursday, August 16, 1962, the first real break in the search for the suspect, deemed by the press "the Slasher," surfaced, with the completion of the composite sketch of Helen's attacker, which had undergone several revisions and input from Helen, who confirmed that the sketch resembled the man who attacked her and left her for dead.

In addition to police releasing the composite sketch, it also appeared on news outlets in Erie and in the *Erie Daily Times* and *Erie Morning News.*

Police went one step further and confirmed more details about Helen's attacker.

He is from 5–10 to six feet in height, weighs between 150 and 180 pounds and may be from eighteen to twenty-five-years-old.

His outstanding features are: blond (almost white) hair, which is closely cut, a thin face, a thin nose which comes from the forehead without a bridge and a pointed, but not prominent chin.

His ears are close to the head and his fingers are long and thin. He is not athletic in appearance.

Also released were details about what Helen's attacker wore:

> *When last seen, the assailant was wearing a striped and long sleeve sweater with a boat neck. The stripes were red, white and a darker color, possibly blue, with red stripes pre-dominant. The stripes run horizontally. He was wearing khaki-colored trousers.*

Detective Sergeant Weir emphasized specifics of the light cream-colored Volkswagen sedan, which had a passenger's assist bar on the dashboard over the glove compartment, a feature known to be present in later models of that type of vehicle.

The release of the composite sketch brought more much-needed leads. One lead caused detectives to confer with investigators from Buffalo, New York, in discussing the possibility that the Knost attack was similar to an attack on a woman in Buffalo on August 29, 1962. The twenty-three-year-old woman was home alone and on the phone with her mother when her attacker climbed through an open window in her bedroom and waited there until she returned to the room, where she was threatened with a knife and sexually assaulted before the perpetrator left through an open window. A suspect was arrested, and detectives prepared photographs, which were shown to Helen.

Of particular importance to detectives was the fact that the description of the Buffalo attacker, according to Weir, was nearly identical to that of Knost's attacker.

Police, hopeful that this could be the break they needed, were disappointed when Helen informed them the Buffalo suspect was not her attacker.

Anxiety around Erie escalated when a forty-nine-year-old woman was found in the administration building of the Port Erie Airport shortly after three o'clock in the morning on Saturday, September 1, 1962. The woman, reportedly found in a dazed condition with her clothes disarranged, spoke incoherently before collapsing on the baggage counter. Sergeant Kenneth Closer and Patrolman Victor Susol from the Millcreek Police Department arrived with paramedics, and the woman was transported to Saint Vincent hospital for internal injuries sustained from the attack.

Speaking with police, the woman said she had been at a downtown Erie barroom and had accepted a ride home with the man who then attacked her. Millcreek Police reached out to the Erie City Police Department, and Detective Sergeant Herman Nowak was asked to assist with the investigation. The victim was unable to furnish a description of the attacker or the vehicle he was driving.

Millcreek police chief Joseph Marshall said the case would have to be checked thoroughly, saying it was too early to even determine if the woman had been attacked in Erie or Millcreek Township. Marshall also said there appeared to be no tie-in to the attack on and abduction of Helen Knost, but detectives from the Erie City Police Department disagreed, noting similarities to the recent assaults on women within the city, including the murder of Laura Mutch and the attack on Clara Carrig. What similarities the detectives were relying on were, however, unknown.

On the surface, this incident should be treated with skepticism, as a conflicting account also appeared in the article "Police Push Hunt for Assailant" in the *Erie Morning News* on September 5, 1962. In this article, Chief Marshall said the forty-nine-year-old victim and her husband had been to a restaurant earlier that evening and that the husband drove the wife home, returning to the restaurant alone. Marshall indicated that from the time the victim was dropped off at home until she appeared at the Port Erie Airport, she could not recall what happened.

By September 5, both detectives from Erie and Millcreek were continuing this investigation; however, no further details were released to the public, and it is believed that the case went cold. Adding to the frustration for detectives were a recent spate of burglaries targeting local businesses. Working together on both the September 1 attack and the recent burglaries, both Erie City deputy chief Chester J. Miller and Millcreek police chief Joseph Marshall expressed confidence in solving these cases.

Toward the end of the month, detectives' attention was directed to the arrest in Rochester, New York, of James Robert Moore, a twenty-eight-year-old landscaper who formerly lived in Erie. Moore had confessed to the September 6, 1962 murder of fourteen-year-old Pamela Moss, confessing he grabbed Moss, strangled and raped her. Afterward, he discarded her body in a water-filled gravel pit. Along with his confession, Moore admitted to sexually molesting at least seventeen other girls, along with raping a nine-year-old. At the time of his arrest, Moore had been on probation in Erie County, New York, following a November 1960 conviction for molesting two girls in the Buffalo suburb of Depew.

Detective Sergeant Weir planned to provide photographs of Moore to Knost to review but did not feel that Moore was responsible for her attack, pointing out that Moore's description and age didn't match Knost's description. Weir was proven correct when Moore was later excluded as a suspect.

As summer gave way to fall, the rewards in all local cases remained unclaimed. In addition to the Knost attack, state police were now faced with the difficulty of another murder, that of twenty-four-year-old gas station attendant Donald Perkins, who was killed at a Mobil-Socony Oil Company gas station on Depot Road in Harborcreek on August 22. This murder would result in another reward being offered to citizens in Erie County, also consisting of $1,000.

The attacks on women resurfaced in the City of Erie. In early October, a nineteen-year-old woman was sexually assaulted by a man whose description matched that of Helen Knost's attacker. The victim, whose name was not released, revealed that she had been persuaded to get into the back of a black Ford sedan. She was then driven to a deserted lakeside area of the city, where she was brutally assaulted and raped before being thrown from the assailant's vehicle. Hospital officials later told Captain Chimenti that the assault had left the girl impregnated.

In November, a fifteen-year-old schoolgirl was also sexually assaulted after accepting a ride from a stranger while returning from classes. The attacker was described as a white male in his late teens to early twenties. Investigators were left struggling to determine if this was related to the slew of other past attacks.

Once again, fewer women appeared on the streets during the day and night. Windows and doors remained locked, and patrols increased within the city as police were once again forced to find a solution to attacks on women that had resurfaced.

As fate would have it, the terror would not subside anytime soon.

CHAPTER 6

SILK STOCKINGS AND DANGEROUS DESIRES

A bitter cold fell on Erie as darkness swept into the neighborhoods on the evening of Monday, December 17, 1962. The light in the second-floor bedroom window of 1018 Washington Place, a two-story cottage-style home, burned into the night. Such a sight was out of the ordinary to nearby resident Margaret Renz, of 1019 Washington Place, who looked on from her own home with growing concern.

It had been almost a week since Renz had heard from her friend, forty-year-old Eleanor Free, the occupant of 1018 Washington Place.

Outside, a fierce wind howled through the streets and sidewalks already covered with a foot of snow.

Concerned, Renz reached out to Eleanor's teenage daughter, who resided with Eleanor's estranged husband in nearby Waterford. After obtaining permission to enter the residence, Margaret contacted a local locksmith, Oliver Kokko, and at eleven o'clock, Margaret, her husband, Harold, and Kokko made their way through the snow to a side door of 1018 Washington Place and entered the home.

Inside, they moved through the first floor, which was in the process of being renovated while Free was on a leave of absence from her job for a minor operation. Free had hoped to complete the renovations soon so she could rent out the other rooms to supplement her income.

As the three made their way upstairs, they spotted the door to one of the bedrooms ajar, with light spilling into the hallway. Pushing the door open, they were met with a sight that made their blood run as cold as the weather outside.

Inside 1018 Washington Place the night Eleanor Free's body was found. *Author's collection.*

Across the street, sixteen-year-old Dennis Renz watched from the window of his home as his mother, father and Oliver Kokko fled Eleanor Free's residence in fear. Dennis Renz would later recount the events to *Erie Times News* reporter Tim Hahn in 2003, remembering, "They told us to stay away."

The Renzes immediately notified police.

Eleanor Free had been murdered.

Patrol Officers Edward Zatynski and Robert Belczyk were the first to arrive, accompanied by Detective Sergeants Herman Nowak and Maurice Sheehan. Within the hour, dozens of police cruisers clogged the snow-filled streets, their lights reflecting off the row of cluttered homes. Deputy Chief Chester Miller arrived, followed by Detective Captain Carl Kalinowski and District Attorney Herbert J. Johnson Jr. and, of course, Erie County coroner Merle Wood.

Inside Eleanor's bedroom, detectives were met with a gruesome sight. Wearing a nightgown and housecoat, Eleanor was lying on her stomach next to her bed on the hardwood floor. Her hands and ankles were tied from behind with electrical cord cut from a portable radio and clock in the bedroom, with the cord fastened to a bedpost. Two nylon stockings were tied together, one end tightened around her neck and the other tied around the knob of the bedroom door. The sweater Eleanor had been wearing was placed over her mouth. Her killer had then apparently torn off a piece of bedsheet, tying it around the sweater like a gag.

Nearby, an electric clock had stopped at 7:47.

Inside the bedroom, blood stained the north and east walls, the windowsills and the door leading into the hallway.

Detective Sergeant Nowak looked to Captain Paul DeDionisio. "It looks like murder."

Eleanor Free was born on June 30, 1922, to James Edward Conroy, a foreman, and Maria Llaveria in Newburgh, New York. Her parents divorced when she was young, and she resided with her mother and two brothers. By 1942, Eleanor had met thirty-three-year-old James Rodgers Free, and she soon became pregnant with their first child, a son. Eleanor married James on January 9, 1943, in Newburgh, New York, while he was stationed at Stewart Air National Guard Base. A daughter soon followed, and around 1950, the Frees moved to Erie, where James worked for the Singer Sewing Machine Company as a manager and later with a local printing firm. At the time of her death, Eleanor had been employed with Lord Manufacturing Company for eleven years as a control tester on third shift.

Top: Eleanor Free. *Erie Morning News*.

Bottom: Investigators inspect Eleanor Free's bedroom. *From left*: District Attorney Johnson, Deputy Chief Miller, Captain Kalinowski and Chief Radaker. *Erie Daily Times*.

Eleanor was visibly beautiful, with a warm smile and blond hair. Many friends and coworkers remembered her "bubbly" personality, kind-hearted nature and affection and love for her children. This made her sudden death all the more shocking that cold December night.

Many of the detectives who entered Eleanor's apartment that night had worked under Captain Chimenti during Laura Mutch's murder investigation, almost two years prior. Now they worked under Carl Kalinowski, and the way Eleanor was found strangled and gagged brought flashbacks of the Mutch murder.

For the moment, however, Chief Radaker arrived and took charge of the investigation.

Late into the night, reporters arrived but were unable to gather enough information before press time. Neighbors, secluded in the warmth of their homes, looked on and gossiped as news spread from house to house. Inside 1018 Washington Place, Coroner Wood pronounced Eleanor Free dead and directed the body to be removed for an autopsy, which indicated that it was clear she had been strangled. Wounds also indicated she had been horribly beaten about the face, chest and body, injured in what Chief Radaker said was a "terrific battle."

Officers and detectives ventured into the cold, knocking on doors and beginning lines of inquiry, starting with the Renz family. Margaret Renz told police Eleanor spent the past Thanksgiving at their home and had recently visited on December 11, staying to watch television before returning home at ten thirty in the evening.

This was the last time police were able to determine that Eleanor had been seen alive.

It was clear to detectives that Eleanor's body showed signs of decomposition, evidence she had likely been dead for several days. Detectives were perplexed that there was no sign of forced entry nor any signs as to how her killer left the home. This indicated, detectives believed, that Eleanor possibly knew her killer. Inside her bedroom, a bloody footprint was found, made by size 10 galoshes. A similar print was located outside the home. Detectives would later remove a portion of the floor with the bloody shoeprint as evidence.

Bloody fingerprints were found on Eleanor's bed and the window shade. Detectives also located a bloodstained paring knife, covered in a woman's scarf, believed to have been used to cut the electrical cord. Detectives so far seemed to exclude burglary as a motive and instead believed it to be a "vengeance style" murder.

The most important pieces of evidence found were two postcards sent to Eleanor; the contents were described as containing "endearing terms," with the writer telling Eleanor that they loved her.

The cards were signed "Mr. X."

Dr. Fust performed the autopsy on Eleanor's body the next day. Dr. Fust noted the numerous bruises and injuries, which included severe marks on her neck. The knot around Eleanor's neck was loose and not tight enough to cause death, possibly placed postmortem. Dr. Fust also located a cut between two of her fingers, which possibly contributed to some of the blood found in the bedroom. Fust confirmed that Eleanor had not been sexually assaulted, and the cause of death was ruled as strangulation. An exact date and time of death could not be cemented, but it was believed that the murder occurred three to six days prior to the body being found.

Eleanor and her husband, James, had been estranged and separated for nearly two years, at Eleanor's request. The morning following the discovery of her body, he arrived at 1018 Washington Place and was later questioned by detectives. James told detectives he had last seen his wife alive on December 6. Following the interrogation of Eleanor's husband, detectives felt the evidence did not support him as her killer; however, he was not immediately eliminated.

Detectives also visited the Lord Manufacturing Plant and questioned Eleanor's coworkers. During this time, detectives were told to question forty-five-year-old Clifford Salow, a friend of Eleanor's.

Detective Sergeants Sheehan and Nowak located Salow at his place of employment and took him to headquarters, where he was questioned for seven hours. Salow admitted to sending the postcards and signing them "Mr. X." Salow's reasoning for signing the cards under the pseudonym was that it was "just one of those things," saying the X symbolized a kiss and was not meant to be mysterious in nature.

Salow said he last saw Eleanor alive on Tuesday, December 11, 1962, around four o'clock in the afternoon, when he brought a prepared dinner to her home. Salow said he only stayed several minutes before leaving. It was then detectives learned Salow had a spare key to Eleanor's home, which raised a red flag. Salow repeatedly denied involvement in Eleanor's murder and denied knowing who murdered her. Chief Radaker later confirmed to reporters that Salow was considered a suspect but had been released later that evening pending further investigation.

Margaret Renz was questioned again by police and mentioned that Eleanor also visited on December 10 for dinner and that the two spent time together that night at a nearby laundromat. Detectives soon cleared Margaret, Harold and Dennis Renz of any involvement.

As the investigation heated up, detectives held firm in the belief that Eleanor knew her killer. Police also believed that either Eleanor let her killer inside willingly or he entered using a spare key. Detectives believed that after leaving Eleanor's home, her killer's clothing must have been covered with blood, based on the struggle that took place in Eleanor's bedroom.

By December 20, 1962, police had questioned some thirty people in the investigation. Detective Captain Kalinowski, upon reviewing the evidence, was comfortable in declaring that robbery and sex had been eliminated as motives for the crime. "Whoever killed Mrs. Free in her home at 1018 Washington Place undoubtedly knew her pretty well and made doubly sure she was dead when he fled," a detective told reporters. "What was the real reason for the killer binding her hands and feet behind her and strangling her with two pairs of nylons together?"

Police also checked the clothing of all individuals questioned for bloodstains.

That same day, Eleanor was laid to rest in a private ceremony at Laurel Hill Cemetery in Millcreek Township. As the detective bureau of the Erie City Police Department processed leads in the case, Deputy Chief Miller conferred with Detective Weir of the state police in Lawrence Park about the possible connection between the murder of Eleanor Free and the attack on Helen Knost.

Sergeant Weir advised Miller that nothing indicated to him both cases were related.

Police again detained James Rodgers Free Sr. for additional questioning. And again, detectives felt confident Free was not involved in his wife's murder. Reporters also learned that "Mr. X" had been identified, checked out thoroughly and released. Detective Captain Kalinowski and Lieutenant Donald Gunter studied fingerprints obtained from the home. Eleanor's fingerprints were also reviewed alongside prints obtained from technicians inside her home. It was on the front page of the *Erie Morning News* that reporters dubbed Eleanor's murder "Silk Stocking" murder.

Clifford Salow was again picked up on the evening of December 21, 1962, and brought in for further questioning behind the closed doors of the detective bureau. Two teams of detectives, along with District Attorney Johnson, participated in the questioning into the early morning hours of December 22 in an attempt to approach the suspect from a new angle to gain additional information. At some point that morning, Safety Director

Hetico, Chief Radaker and other top police officials were also involved in the questioning.

Salow was again released and not charged.

Following Salow's release, more men and women were questioned: neighbors, more coworkers and just about anyone and everyone who might have known or had a relationship with Eleanor.

As for Kalinowski, he kept coming back to who he felt was the prime suspect in the case, though he refused to name him publicly. "He was running around with her," Kalinowski told *Erie Times News* reporter Tim Hahn in 2003. "He followed her all the time. He knew every move she made."

Kalinowski was determined to see Eleanor's killer brought to justice and promised the investigation was not about to stop, even as police closed in on fifty persons questioned in the investigation. As for the *Erie Daily Times*, it declared on December 24 that the investigation had come to a standstill, with no plans to question anyone further in the seven-day-old case.

The *Erie Daily Times* reported:

> *In essence, detectives are continuing to question acquaintances of Mrs. Free, but they apparently have nothing substantial enough to bring anyone into headquarters.*

The intense flurry of activity within the department gradually returned to normal, despite teams of detectives still hard at work on the case.

Soon, the case faded from the front pages as the city turned to the Christmas holiday and other news.

The *Times*, reviewing the city payrolls, pointed to the troubling fact that the Erie City Police Department was understaffed, due in part to cutbacks in personnel. This was a change since the leadership under former police chief Edward Williams, who attempted to have twenty-five additional policeman for the department to be considered full strength. The payroll study also showed that other departments in the city had suffered cutbacks, something that created concern among local lawmakers.

By the ninth day of the investigation, detectives circled back to the same belief that Eleanor was murdered by someone who either knew her or monitored every detail of her life. Additional chemical tests ordered by Coroner Wood also failed to disclose any additional evidence pointing to her killer, and Wood proceeded with signing the death certificate.

The day after Christmas found detectives believing a break was imminent and confirming to the *Times* that Clifford Salow had already been interrogated twice, once in the presence of the district attorney, and that they intended to interrogate him again. Police also acknowledged that a polygraph device would possibly be requested by detectives to help in the investigation.

As for Clifford Salow, everything led back to him—circumstantially, at least.

On December 28, 1962, Coroner Wood announced plans to call an inquest if police were able to develop a prime suspect. While police focused on Salow, detectives also undertook a closer examination of the stockings used to strangle Eleanor. As reporters prodded for additional details, investigators remained tight-lipped about any involvement with the state police and their polygraph machine.

Later that day, police picked up Clifford Salow and transported him to the Erie County Courthouse, where Eleanor's husband also had been taken for additional questioning. Before questioning Salow, police indicated they had evidence that showed he visited Eleanor's residence on December 12. This evidence, along with Salow's inconsistent statements, gave detectives the upper hand.

Present when Salow was given the polygraph examination was Corporal Frank W. Lesch of the state police, Chief Radaker, Deputy Chief Miller, Detective Captain Kalinowski and District Attorney Johnson. The exact results of Salow's polygraph examination remain unknown; however, during questioning, Salow confessed that on December 12, 1962, he entered Eleanor's residence with a spare key and, after entering Eleanor's bedroom, found her deceased and tied up. Salow claimed he panicked and left immediately, heading downtown to Tenth and State Streets before going to a store, then finally returning home, keeping his discovery a secret.

At one point, Kalinowski took over during the interrogation. It was then that Salow began to exhibit an unusual range of emotions, from sobbing to screaming, only to then pound his fists on the table in despair.

"We had him on the ropes," Kalinowski later reminisced. "We worked real hard for a while, and then he couldn't talk. We ran up a brick wall, and all of a sudden it was dropped."

Salow asked for an attorney, and the interrogation ended on December 29, 1962.

Despite coming up short with a confession, evidence allowed detectives to narrow down the possible date of death to either December 11 or 12. Although Salow's right to an attorney did not necessarily shield him from responsibility in the crime or any possible charges, his statement that he located Eleanor's body and failed to report it indicated the possibility of withholding evidence, considered a felony according to District Attorney Johnson. Discussions were had about whether or not Salow should be charged.

"This is a toughie," District Attorney Johnson expressed, discussing the next steps of the investigation. "We'll pursue every possible avenue of evidence in solving the case."

While District Attorney Johnson declined to confirm the possibility of additional polygraph examinations, several more witnesses were questioned, with Johnson strongly emphasizing that those questioned were not considered suspects and were friends of Eleanor's. With that, nearly two weeks after her mangled body was found tied up inside her bedroom, police were no closer to arresting a prime suspect in Eleanor's murder. Rumors abounded about persons believed to be next in line to receive polygraph examinations; however, they were ignored by the police and the district attorney.

The year 1962 came to an end without an arrest or charges, and on January 3, 1963, city hall announced the possibility of a reward: "Inasmuch as the police appear to be up against a stone wall, offering of a reward may do a lot of good in helping to solve the mysterious case."

The *Erie Daily Times* was quick to mention that the reward in Laura Mutch's murder still remained unclaimed. With three teams of detectives still assigned to the investigation of Eleanor's murder, police branched out with further questioning, including interviews with two of Eleanor's female friends from Rochester, New York, in the hope that detectives could obtain information that might have been overlooked.

With more than 130 persons interviewed, boxes of evidence and what seemed to be endless records—and with no end in sight—police had been unable to address any further suspects in Eleanor's murder. Deputy Chief Miller indicated he felt that once a definitive motive had been established, this would help crack the case. District Attorney Johnson elaborated on new leads that produced more names to be questioned.

A check at the prothonotary's office at the Erie County Courthouse revealed that Eleanor had filed a suit for divorce against her husband on July 13, 1962, with the divorce papers served by Constable Anthony DeSanti on July 18, 1961, at six-thirty in the evening, at 1018 Washington Place. The divorce action, of course, was never completed.

Again forced back to the drawing board, detectives determined the blood type found in Eleanor's home and reinvestigated the bloodstained paring knife and other evidence. Detectives also believed that the stockings were tied around Eleanor's neck postmortem and that this was not the cause of her strangulation.

1018 Washington Place as it looks today. *Author's collection.*

Grave of Eleanor Free, Laurel Hill Cemetery. *Author's collection.*

Chief Radaker believed this was supported by evidence that Eleanor fought her attacker. Radaker himself believed Eleanor had simply been caught by surprise, choked and physically beaten by her killer, but not before fighting back valiantly. Once dead, she was then dragged across the floor, tied with the nylon stockings and left hanging from the doorknob.

Several weeks later, the Security Peoples Trust Company, administrator of Eleanor's estate, filed a damage claim against Erie County for the portions of wall and flooring removed as evidence. Attorney David S. Gifford submitted a bill for $600 on behalf of the estate in damages. Then county solicitor Lindley M. McClelland said he did not feel the responsibility fell on the county to reimburse these costs and asked for a bill of particulars. A similar claim was also filed against the city. The county eventually decided that it would not pay the damages.

Detectives remained convinced that they knew the identity of Eleanor's killer, but without further evidence, they were unable to bring him to justice. And with the police no closer to an arrest in the case, 1018 Washington Place remained eerily vacant as the weeks wore on.

CHAPTER 7

A CORPSE IN
AX MURDER HOLLOW

D an Skala's car plowed through the snow-covered street and into the driveway of 604 Crotty Drive around noon on January 20, 1963. The phone call he had received minutes before seemed ominous. David Crotty—Skala's sister-in-law Martha's husband—said something serious had happened, and he requested Skala's presence as soon as possible, adding not to say anything to anyone else, including Skala's wife.

Skala entered the Crotty home and was plunged into instant pandemonium. Martha Crotty—the sister of Dan's wife, Jessie—stood next to her husband, David, who was on the phone. Some of their children were also present. The look on David Crotty's face said it all: the look of a frightened father.

David Crotty's gaze then connected with Skala's.

"I can't understand," Crotty said, frustrated, holding the phone out to Skala. "Would you take this call? Tell me what name they're going to give as the name of the boy that Lynn was out with?"

Skala took the phone and introduced himself to the person on the other end, a young female named Paulette Cywinski. Figuring it had something to do with his niece, Mary Lynn, known by friends and family simply as Lynn, Skala was in the dark as to what was happening but continued the conversation with Paulette, asking for the name of the boy Lynn was out with.

Skala obtained two names: John Harvey and Daniel Biebighausen.

Or maybe it was Biebighauser?

Paulette wasn't entirely sure of the spelling or pronunciation, to be honest. But that was the least of anyone's concerns as Skala hung up the phone and soon found himself thumbing through a nearby telephone directory to try to locate the names.

Skala found a similar name and dialed the number but was unable to reach anyone, listening in frustration to an endless dial tone. Skala hung up and turned to his brother-in-law in an attempt to figure out what was going on.

David told him he had gone to church that morning at nine thirty, returning an hour later. As David reached the front door, his wife informed him that twenty-year-old Lynn never returned home the night before after going out with a friend from Edinboro College. After locating the phone number for Lynn's friend Paulette, both David and Martha phoned her, asking where Lynn was. The Crottys were faced with confusion when it was learned that Paulette told her parents she stayed at Lynn's house the night prior.

Confused and emotional, Paulette expressed to Lynn's parents that she did not want to get involved with what was going on, in case the newspapers got involved. This incensed David Crotty, whose concern was turning to anger as he found himself unable to locate his daughter. David told Paulette that Lynn never returned home.

Lynn Crotty had disappeared.

John Floyd Harvey and Daniel Roy Biebighauser arrived at the Crotty home just after one o'clock that afternoon, after locating it in the phone book. Confronted by Lynn's parents and Dan Skala, both Harvey and Biebighauser were questioned about Lynn's whereabouts. Harvey, Crotty testified several months later, did most of the talking. Biebighauser, he said, "didn't explain anything unless I practically dug it out of him."

Harvey told Lynn's parents that Biebighauser told him Lynn wasn't feeling well and took her home, dropping her off on Smithson Avenue, about a block away, sometime between three thirty and four in the morning.

David Crotty asked Biebighauser about the exact route he had taken to bring his daughter home. Biebighauser said he traveled across Route 5 before turning up Smithson Avenue, which is where he let Lynn out of his vehicle before reversing back onto Route 5. Nothing seemed suspicious to David Crotty, but there was still the nagging thought that he was not getting the answers he and Lynn's family deserved.

Lynn's father continued to fire off question after question at Biebighauser. What condition was she in when she was dropped off? Had she fallen? Did she have bruises on her? How ill was she, exactly? Biebighauser remained

Daniel Roy Biebighauser. *Author's collection.*

tight-lipped, responding with short answers, only adding that Lynn was throwing up when he dropped her off.

Seeing he was getting nowhere, Crotty sent one of his sons to the home of Lewis Penman. David looked on from the front window, watching his son sprint through the heavy snow, disappearing around the corner.

Deep down, David Crotty's stomach sank deeper and deeper.

Lewis Penman had just finished his Sunday dinner when he received a visit at his front door from the youngest son of the Crotty family. David Crotty was requesting Penman come to his home as soon as possible. A detective sergeant with the Pennsylvania State Police stationed at the Lawrence Park Barracks, Penman had been spending his day off with family when he was requested to go to the Crotty home.

A native of Manor, Pennsylvania, Penman worked for the Pennsylvania Railroad Police Department before graduating from the state police academy in Hershey, where he received training at the intelligence school in Fort Knox, Kentucky. World War II saw him working for the U.S. Army Intelligence Division as an investigator in the Allied Control Mission in Bulgaria before returning to the United States.

Detective Penman knew the Crotty family and regarded their reputation as being stellar in the local community. Such a request from David Crotty was certainly unusual, as Penman would later recall. Slipping his arms into his coat, Penman ventured outside and, because of the heavy snowfall, decided to drive the block over to the Crotty home.

Penman arrived several minutes later and entered through the door off Emmett Drive, where he was met by David and Martha Crotty. Penman was almost overwhelmed with information. In order to gain a clearer understanding about what transpired, he ordered everyone other than Lynn's parents out of the basement recreation room. Penman was told that Lynn had gone out the night before on a double date and failed to come home. For the next thirty minutes, he spoke with other family members before being informed that Harvey and Biebighauser were waiting upstairs.

Penman had Crotty send one of the men down to speak with him.

John Floyd Harvey lumbered down the steps, and the two spoke about what happened the night before as Penman jotted down Harvey's statement on a tablet. Harvey told Penman that he and Biebighauser, a coworker from the R.M. Kerner Company, had gone out for the first time together, with both men meeting Harvey's girlfriend, Paulette Cywinski, who had coordinated a double date. Harvey last saw Biebighauser and Lynn around

The Pilot House. *Erie County Historical Society.*

four o'clock that morning in front of Biebighauser's apartment at 2612½ Parade Street. Penman thoroughly dissected Harvey's statement and, after an hour, sent him back upstairs.

Daniel Biebighauser came down next, with Penman again introducing himself. From the onset, Biebighauser admitted to being a married man despite having gone out on a date with Lynn the night before. Biebighauser told Penman he met Lynn and Paulette at the Villa in Cambridge Springs. Because the girls were underage, they were refused service, and the parties decided to head to downtown Erie, going to the Pilot House. Biebighauser drove to Erie with Harvey; Paulette and Lynn followed.

The four of them arrived at the Pilot House and stayed for the floor show while taking in a few drinks. When the floor show was over, they traveled to the Wesleyville Athletic Club in Wesleyville. When the parties left for Wesleyville, Lynn rode with Biebighauser while Harvey drove Paulette. After arriving at the athletic club, they again had several drinks and listened to the band until approximately three thirty in the morning.

From there, they went to their vehicles, where Lynn removed her items from Paulette's vehicle, placing them into Biebighauser's. Biebighauser then followed Paulette to his apartment on Parade Street. Biebighauser told Penman that, at the moment, he resided with his wife and son at 2326½ Liberty Street but had recently signed a lease for the apartment on Parade Street.

Biebighauser also told Penman he had given the keys to the apartment to Harvey earlier on.

After arriving at the apartment, both cars parked against the curb. Biebighauser attempted to put his arm around Lynn and kiss her. Lynn, however, did not reciprocate and shied away from him. Biebighauser claimed he did not force the issue and that ten or fifteen minutes later, she told him she was not feeling well and wanted to go home. Biebighauser pulled up alongside Paulette's vehicle and told her and Harvey he was taking Lynn home.

Biebighauser said he drove on Parade Street before performing a U-turn and heading north on Parade until reaching East Sixth Street; there, he took a right turn and continued eastbound until reaching Lawrence Park, with Lynn providing directions along the way. Biebighauser remembered reaching the last blinking light in Lawrence Park before turning right and driving on until Lynn told him to stop and let her out, which he did. Biebighauser acknowledged not waiting to see if Lynn made it home safely and could not recall which direction she walked off in, but he did recall seeing Lynn vomit.

Biebighauser returned to his apartment on Parade Street and woke Harvey up. After getting the keys from him, he told Harvey he was going home, drove to his apartment on Liberty Street around six thirty in the morning and went to bed. Just as with Harvey's statement, Penman found no discrepancies, and he later remembered Harvey and Biebighauser as being cooperative and willing to provide information.

With family coming and going, confusion reigned in the Crotty house as Penman struggled to plot his next steps. Dan Skala, who had left to get his wife, Jessie, had returned. Jessie Skala immediately approached Biebighauser, attempting to pepper him with questions about her niece.

"Why would you leave a girl off a block away from her home? What kind of a man are you, to do a thing like that?" Jessie demanded angrily.

Looking away, Biebighauser shrugged his shoulders, stating that he only did what Lynn asked him to do. "She was ill because she had been drinking."

"What did she drink?"

"What was it?" Biebighauser turned to Harvey, looking for an answer.

Before either could respond, Jessie Skala continued: "Don't you know what you were drinking?"

Harvey said he believed Lynn had a vodka, a glass of tomato juice and a rum and coke.

Penman learned from Lynn's older brother that he had locked the house at midnight. Lynn, not having an extra key, could have easily found the home locked and instead gone to the home of a girlfriend or nearby neighbor. Reviewing his notes, Penman was not able to come up with anything that would lead him closer to locating Lynn.

Penman called Harvey and Biebighauser back into the basement and questioned them together. Penman noted that both men seemed concerned about the whereabouts of Lynn and what had happened to her. Nothing gave him any indication he should suspect either of having been involved in anything nefarious.

Penman told both men he knew they were married and that the situation they found themselves in was not a good one. Despite his initial beliefs, Penman told them he felt they knew—or knew someone who knew—what happened to Lynn. Penman informed both men that they had an hour to contact their friends and anyone who knew Lynn. They were to find any clue they could about what happened to her.

As Detective Penman finished speaking with both men, Dan Skala spoke to some of Lynn's siblings and concocted a plan to search nearby lots in the area to see if there was any trace of Lynn. They managed to cover four or five blocks in the frigid weather before returning empty-handed.

By then, Harvey, Biebighauser and Detective Penman were gone.

After Biebighauser and Harvey's departure, Penman reached out to the chief of police in Lawrence Park, notifying him of Lynn's disappearance. Lawrence Park police requested Pennsylvania state police to assist in the investigation to locate Lynn, and Penman then followed up with his superior Detective Sergeant Leo Weir. Both men decided to pursue the investigation further to provide any additional assistance necessary.

Penman then left for the Cywinski home, arriving at seven thirty in the evening. After speaking with Paulette and her parents, Penman learned that Biebighauser and Harvey had been there prior to his arrival, trying to find Lynn. Penman spent the next hour gathering the names of Lynn's college associates, friends and other people unknown to Lynn's parents. Penman left at nine o'clock and spent hours, into the early morning of January 21, attempting to reach anyone he could.

After just a few hours' sleep, Detective Penman had a conference that morning with Detective Sergeant Weir and Ed Strong of the Lawrence Park police to review the case. It became clear that they were no closer to being able to locate Lynn, and they decided to question Harvey and Biebighauser once more.

Police arrived at the R.M. Kerner Company at nine thirty and learned that Biebighauser had failed to show up to work. The men then left for the residence of John Harvey and spoke with him for an hour and a half before heading to Biebighauser's Liberty Street apartment. After speaking to Biebighauser's wife, Louise, they learned that Biebighauser had left at ten thirty for work. Believing Biebighauser's employers misunderstood their inquiries, they backtracked and revisited the R.M. Kerner Company; on their arrival, they were informed that Louise Biebighauser had called, reporting her husband was home.

The detectives returned, again, to Biebighauser's Liberty Street apartment, parking behind a red 1962 Ford Galaxie 500. Weir and Strong waited in the car as Penman climbed the stairs to the second floor and introduced himself again to Biebighauser. Penman told Biebighauser he wanted to review his previous statement at the Lawrence Park Police Department. Biebighauser agreed to leave with detectives.

As Penman and Biebighauser exited the apartment, Penman asked Biebighauser if he was the owner of the Ford Galaxie. Biebighauser confirmed he was, and Penman asked for permission to search the vehicle. "No, I'll be glad to have you look through it," Biebighauser said, handing the keys over to Penman.

Penmen opened the front passenger door and searched the glove compartment. Under the front passenger seat, he found a cigar box. Opening the box, Penman found two folded pieces of paper. Removing the papers, Penman unfolded them and was faced with two pencil sketches of nude women in frightening poses.

Penman felt like he had been punched in the gut.

Staggering back from the car, Penman looked to Biebighauser and motioned to the pieces of paper, asking who had drawn them. Biebighauser admitted to having done the artwork and said he previously studied art. Penman brushed past Biebighauser and opened the trunk, performing a hasty examination. Penman then asked Biebighauser again if he would voluntarily leave with him for the department.

Biebighauser nodded his head in the affirmative.

The detectives and Biebighauser set off for the Lawrence Park Police Department, but because of mechanical problems, they did not arrive until after two fifteen.

At the Lawrence Park Police Department, the men headed for the conference room. Penman wasted no time in getting down to business, asking Biebighauser to repeat his statement with Weir and Strong present.

As Biebighauser retold his story, Penman asked Biebighauser for his wallet, a practice he was known for when he harbored suspicions about someone. While going through the wallet, Penman found a sales slip dated January 21 from the Sportsman store in West Erie Plaza for the purchase of a firearm.

Asking Biebighauser to continue providing his statement to Weir and Strong, Penman slipped out of the room and rang the Sportsman store. Penman confirmed the store still had the carbon copy of the receipt, which was for the purchase of a handgun that had taken place that morning between nine thirty and ten. Penman finished the call and returned to the conference room, listening as Biebighauser finished his statement.

Once Biebighauser finished his statement, Detective Sergeant Weir left the room. Penman questioned Biebighauser about the receipt for the handgun. Biebighauser said he purchased the gun that morning for the protection of his wife and son for the family's upcoming move to the new apartment on Parade Street, because the neighborhood was bad. Biebighauser confirmed his wife was unaware of the purchase, as he had not informed her of it, and confirmed he did not have the firearm in his possession.

The absence of the firearm after purchase was not out of the ordinary at the time, due to Pennsylvania state law. When a firearm was purchased, the buyer would receive a receipt and then fill out an application, with possession not being allowed for three days afterward in accordance with state law. Following the completion of the application, it would then be forwarded to the state police in Harrisburg through either the Erie County Sherriff's Department or the Erie City Police Department.

Penman had had enough at this point and was not falling for Biebighauser's story. There was something he was holding back.

"You know and I know what happened to Lynn Crotty," Penman said to Biebighauser.

An eerie silence hung between both men. The only sound was the ticking of a wall clock.

"Yes, she's dead," Biebighauser said, dropping his head. "I killed her."

It was 3:14 p.m.

The words hit Penman like a sledgehammer.

"How? Why? When?" Penman asked, his voice betraying his eagerness to find out more information. "Are you sure?"

Changing his story again, Biebighauser said that during the early morning hours of January 20, he left his Parade Street apartment and was driving eastbound on East Thirty-Eighth Street when Lynn became sick and asked him to stop the car. As soon as he stopped the vehicle, Lynn opened the door and vomited outside. It was then, according to Biebighauser, that he started to shake, having the chills before blacking out.

Biebighauser regained consciousness and found Lynn in the back seat of his car. Biebighauser removed her from the back seat and placed her in the trunk before driving back to his Parade Street apartment, where he sat in front of the building for ten or fifteen minutes before leaving, this time traveling westbound on West Thirty-Eighth Street. At the intersection with Sterrettania Road, Biebighauser took a left and traveled south before dumping Lynn's body in the woods.

Penman left the conference room and informed Detective Weir of Biebighauser's confession. Weir and Penman reentered the conference room, and after a brief discussion, Biebighauser told detectives he would take them to Lynn's body.

It was four thirty in the afternoon when Weir, Penman and Sergeant Strong left the department with Biebighauser. Within several minutes, they arrived on East Thirty-Eighth Street in the vicinity of St. John Kanty College. As they drove west, Biebighauser pointed to the side of the road.

"This is where it happened."

The car skidded to a halt in the snow, and Weir exited the vehicle to retrieve what appeared to be a garment bag from the side of the road. After Weir climbed back into the vehicle, they traveled west until they reached the intersection of West Thirty-Eighth Street and Sterrettania Road. Turning south, they passed the desolate, snow-covered fields and barren woodlots of the countryside, well beyond the city limits.

At a certain point in the roadway, Biebighauser, calmly looking out the window, told detectives they had missed the road. Detective Sergeant Weir stopped and turned around, backtracking to Thomas Road. For those who were born and raised in Erie, however, Thomas Road had a more sinister name.

Ax Murder Hollow.

A noted lover's lane, Ax Murder Hollow was forever intertwined with tales of superstition and a legend that revolved around a farmer who brutally murdered his unfaithful wife and their children with an ax somewhere in the dark woods. Local teenagers and thrill seekers claimed the ghost of the jilted farmer haunted the area, murdering those he came across. Since the 1940s, the legend had spiraled into an almost mythical yet still frightening story, one not lost on detectives that night.

Biebighauser directed the detectives about seven-tenths of a mile down Thomas Road until he pointed to the northern side of the road, where a

East Thirty-Eighth Street, looking west, where Biebighauser murdered Mary Lynn Crotty. *Author's collection.*

Present-day location of Ax Murder Hollow on Thomas Road; the approximate area where Biebighauser discarded Mary Lynn's body. *Author's collection.*

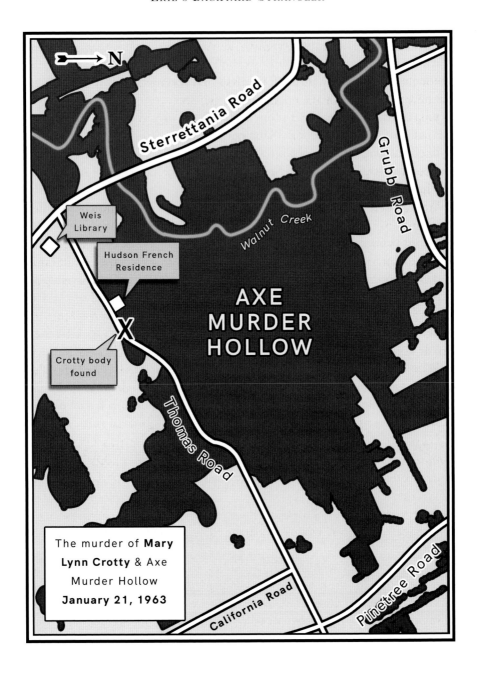

N

Sterrettania Road

Grubb Road

Walnut Creek

Weis Library

Hudson French Residence

AXE MURDER HOLLOW

Crotty body found

Thomas Road

The murder of **Mary Lynn Crotty** & Axe Murder Hollow **January 21, 1963**

California Road

Pinetree Road

large fallen tree was covered with snow. Weir stopped, the tires crunching against the ice- and snow-covered gravel road. As he exited the vehicle, the headlights shined eerily through the trees. The occupants sat inside the car, listening to the hum of the engine as they waited.

Weir ventured off the road, plunging into the deep snow. He circled around the fallen log pointed out by Biebighauser, maintaining a careful distance before returning to the vehicle. Once behind the wheel, he exchanged a glance with Strong and Penman. No words needed to be said.

Their worst fears had been confirmed.

Weir turned the car around and drove back up the road until he reached the home of Hudson French at 5559 Thomas Road. Weir knocked on the front door of the French residence and asked to use their telephone. Several minutes later, the group drove back to the intersection of Thomas and Sterrettania Roads, where they waited for the arrival of the coroner and a photographer.

Coroner Merle Wood received a phone call from Major Russell Knies of the state police notifying him he was requested at Sterrettania and Thomas Roads, near where a body had been located. Coroner Wood, along with one of his assistants, drove out to meet detectives, arriving there shortly after five o'clock. Also arriving around this time were additional personnel from the state police and Robert Nelson, a local photographer.

Soon, the procession of about four or five cars traveled to where Biebighauser dumped Lynn's body. Weir, whose vehicle was at the front, stopped when he spotted a garment on the side of the road. Weir exited, retrieved the garment and then proceeded to the crime scene, where he placed the vehicle in park.

Penman asked where the remains were in proximity to the log.

"Behind there," Biebighauser responded in a low voice, pointing directly at the log.

A cold wind bristled through the trees as Coroner Wood and others looked on. Robert Nelson took photographs from a distance before nodding to Wood. Coroner Wood trudged through the snow toward the fallen tree, still partially covered with snow. As he inched closer, about thirty feet from the road, Wood spotted exposed portions of what appeared to be a body wedged against the fallen tree. As police looked on, Coroner Wood directed his assistant to carefully remove snow from around the body. The body was completely nude save for a handkerchief or scarf tied around the left wrist. Once Lynn's body was removed, several stab and slash wounds were spotted, which were noted to detectives at the scene. After Lynn's body was

Detective Penman inspects Biebighauser's Ford Galaxie. *Author's collection.*

transported to the Erie County Morgue, police searched the area for any weapons and evidence.

After a search was performed of the area and scene photographs were completed, Penman, Weir and Sergeant Strong left with Biebighauser, returning to the state police barracks in Lawrence Park. Biebighauser was fed and then interrogated by Detective Sergeant Weir, Sergeant Strong and District Attorney Johnson.

As darkness fell on Lawrence Park and Biebighauser was interrogated, Detective Penman traveled to Biebighauser's apartment on Liberty Street and had the 1962 Ford Galaxie removed to the state police barracks for a more thorough inspection.

During the early morning hours of January 22, 1963, word spread throughout Erie of the grisly murder. A languid Major Russell Knies spoke to reporters around one o'clock in the morning, confirming some similarities between the murder of Lynn Crotty and the cases of Helen Knost and Laura Mutch.

The state police confirmed they were looking into the possible connection between the three cases.

Before the news spread, Dan Skala was notified of Biebighauser's confession and arrest. Lynn's body, he was told, had been recovered. Skala took the heavy responsibility of breaking the news to the family, an experience that would haunt him for the rest of his life. He never wanted to experience such a tragedy again.

Skala praised the work done by Detectives Penman and Weir, as well as those who assisted in the investigation. "You have to hand it to them," Skala told the *Erie Morning News*. "These boys have been through it so many times. They know how to handle a difficult situation."

After being informed of Lynn's death that night, David Crotty reportedly confronted Biebighauser at the station. Upon seeing Biebighauser, his emotions reached a climax, and Crotty lunged after him, having to be restrained by three police officers. Biebighauser reportedly looked on with the same unemotional response and blank stare as before.

That morning, Erie awoke to the following headline: "Erie Machinist, 21, Admits Slaying Lawrence Park Girl."

The Crotty family finally was able to find Lynn, but the wounds her murder inflicted on them would be more painful than they could imagine, a pain that lingers to this day.

Mary Lynn Crotty was born on May 2, 1942, to David J. Crotty and Martha Kennedy in Erie, Pennsylvania. A sophomore at Edinboro College,

Lynn was majoring in primary grade teaching. In addition to being attractive, she was well liked and respected by those who knew her.

Lynn was remembered as "an average girl from a nice family," according to Harry K. Rhodes, supervising principal of Lawrence Park Township School District. "Lynn was the type anyone would be proud to call the girl next door, the babysitter, or just a friend."

Lynn and her twin brother, David, were the oldest of seven Crotty children who grew up in Lawrence Park and lived most of their lives on Crotty Drive, named after Lynn's father, who helped develop the area.

Mary Lynn Crotty. *Author's collection.*

In high school, Lynn stood out as a proud member of the Future Teachers of America Club, Y-Teens, the Spanish Club and the yearbook staff. Entering Edinboro College in the fall of 1961, Lynn belonged to the Student Pennsylvania State Education Association. As Lynn's grieving family planned for her funeral, her fall school schedule, which she had excitedly worked so hard toward, was never fulfilled.

Louise Biebighauser had been blindsided by her husband's arrest. "He is a quiet boy," Louise told an *Erie Morning News* reporter.

Hearing of her husband's arrest, Louise prepared to leave the apartment with her six-month-old son as soon as possible, packing only the essentials to stay temporarily with her parents.

Reporters descended upon the apartment before she could leave, hounding her with questions. "I can't understand it." Louise, holding her son, shook her head in disbelief. "We were happy. There was never any trouble of any kind and Dan never saw anyone else that I know of."

Louise Biebighauser left the apartment, vowing never to return.

Mary Lynn Crotty's autopsy was performed by Dr. John Fust that morning at Hamot Hospital at about ten o'clock. Dr. Fust would list Lynn's injuries, according to the autopsy report:

> *Little pin-point or puncture wounds of the skin of the forehead and of the nose, of the right upper eyelid. There was a streak of blood from the left corner of the mouth and dried on the left cheek. There was abrasion of the skin of the chin. There were linear abrasions in the anterior and lateral skin of the neck, and imprints in the skin of the neck posteriorly.*

Dr. Fust would testify at Biebighauser's trial to the gruesome injuries inflicted on Lynn:

> *There were numerous stab wounds of the chest that ranged from one-eighth of an inch to one and one-quarter inches in length. Most of them were about an eighth to a quarter of an inch in length. Four of them were in the upper chest near the breastbone. There was one above the right breast, four in the middle portion of the right breast, three above the nipple of the left breast and two below it. And the largest, one and one-quarter inch laceration lay about halfway between the left nipple and the navel in the left upper quarter of the abdomen. There was a slight abrasion of the middle surface of the left thigh, and there were imprints in the skin such as might have been made by twigs or branches or stones. Blood stained the skin and the mucous membranes of the vulva and of the upper middle portions of the thigh. There was a small—I shouldn't say "small"—there was, well, it was a small abrasion of the vaginal mucosa on the left, just inside the opening of the vagina and bloody fluid lay in the vagina.*

The wounds on Lynn's neck, according to Dr. Fust, were linear imprints caused by pressure from cloth, a fine rope or wire. Because the knife wounds to Lynn's body bore no signs of hemorrhaging in the wounds themselves, Dr. Fust determined these were caused postmortem. Dr. Fust concluded that Lynn died from asphyxia due to strangulation and believed that the knife wounds and stab marks were caused by a weapon similar to a pen knife.

Lynn's murder added a gruesome footnote to the legend of Ax Murder Hollow.

By 1963, Thomas Road was considered the least traveled road in Millcreek Township and certainly was not a location that stood out in the area. As dusk descended on Thomas Road on the evening of January 22, 1963, *Erie Morning News* reporter Tom McCormack ventured out to the desolate area. Accompanying him were a photographer and the city editor.

The group reached the approximate area where police had been the night before, parking their press cars off the side of the road. Thomas Road had been plowed when McCormack and the others arrived. In describing the scene, McCormack wrote that the snow there was "clean and pure," unlike the snow in the city. Surveying the area where Lynn Crotty's body was found, McCormack described the area in almost poetic prose:

> *The drifted snow lay along the roadside and stretched through the woods peacefully, softly, unbroken, like a blanket that shrouds a dark secret.*

Erie Morning News reporter Tom McCormack kneels down next to the log where Lynn Crotty's body was found. *Erie Morning News.*

McCormack noted the eerie isolation, saying no other cars traveled the road while they were there. McCormack's mind was immediately thrust back to the legends of the area. "The tales say birds seldom sing here," McCormack wrote. "None was singing yesterday."

It was then that the newspapermen spotted the fallen log and, surrounding it, the snowfall, impacted and broken by footprints. Thirty-eight feet from the road, McCormack crouched next to the log, envisioning what had taken place there. Fifteen feet away, he looked toward the edge of the earth that dropped into a deep ravine.

The crime scene was confirmed to the newspapermen when several specks of blood, still frozen in the snow, were found. The realization set in among them that the location was the perfect spot to hide a body, which could have been well concealed for years and not be seen.

With daylight fading, a cold front descended on the area, and the men departed from the dreary, darkened landscape of Ax Murder Hollow.

Daniel Roy Biebighauser was arraigned before Alderman Michael Kinecki at seven fifteen in the evening and charged with Lynn Crotty's murder. Detectives of the Erie City Police Department saw Crotty's murder as an opportunity to breathe new life into the Mutch and Carrig cases. Although he was not a suspect in the murder of Eleanor Free, Biebighauser was now on the radar of local detectives, who planned to question him concerning that attack.

"We are closely investigating Miss Crotty's murder for a possible connection with some of these other cases," acknowledged Major Russell Knies of the state police.

District Attorney Johnson echoed the statement from Major Knies, telling reporters, "I won't say we have ruled out the possibility of an association between these crimes."

While speaking with Biebighauser, detectives became alarmed when he willingly confessed to also sexually assaulting a sixteen-year-old girl. This was confirmed when the victim provided a statement to detectives on January 24.

It was around nine o'clock in the evening on December 3, 1962, when sixteen-year-old Nancy Wierzbicki stood on the corner of Eighteenth and State Streets with a fifteen-year-old male friend named Joe. Wierzbicki spotted Daniel Biebighauser, with whom she had gone on a date that past November.

Wierzbicki called out to Biebighauser, who spotted her and parked his vehicle in a nearby lot. After some small talk, Wierzbicki got into Biebighauser's vehicle with Joe. Nancy's friend asked to pick up a friend on Sixth and State, and after the pickup, Biebighauser returned to Eighteenth and State, dropped off the two young men and then traveled to a drugstore on Eighteenth and Parade, where he and Nancy purchased two bottles of pop.

From there, Biebighauser and Wierzbicki went to East Tenth, between Holland and German Streets, where Biebighauser ran inside and got a glass cup. He soon returned and drove out to South Gore Road, near Route 97 in Millcreek Township.

Biebighauser, who had a bottle of vodka, drank straight from the bottle, while Nancy mixed hers with orange pop as the two of them talked. Biebighauser attempted to make advances toward Nancy, but she had begun to feel sick from the alcohol, and at some point, she opened the door to get some fresh air.

Nancy became worse as she sat back in the car. She opened the door again, vomiting onto the ground. After she was able to compose herself, Nancy sat back in the seat, and then Biebighauser suddenly struck her across the throat. Nancy was clutching her throat, struggling to breathe, when

Detective Penman (*left*) walks alongside Daniel Roy Biebighauser following his arraignment. *Author's collection.*

Biebighauser pounced on her, his hands around her throat. She pressed against the steering wheel, breaking it while trying to press the horn.

Nancy then blacked out.

She regained consciousness in the back seat of Biebighauser's car. Her hands were tied behind her back and her feet fettered together with her nylon stockings. A rag, shoved into her mouth, prevented her from screaming. Nancy lost consciousness again. When she came to, her dress, brassiere and underwear were torn and in disarray, with Biebighauser next to her.

Removing his pants, Biebighauser climbed on top of her and started to rape her.

His voice growled with anger, as if in a daze. "You fucked him, didn't you! You fucked him!"

Nancy wriggled her feet free and started to cry, pleading to be let go. Biebighauser removed the rag from her mouth.

"If you scream I'm going to kill you," he said in a monotone. Nancy glanced down to see a pocketknife pressed against her ribs.

"I won't scream," Nancy stuttered, quivering with fear.

After several minutes, Biebighauser dropped his head.

"I'm sorry," Biebighauser mumbled as he leaned over, cutting the stockings from her wrists.

Nancy grabbed her coat, cloaking herself as she scooted into the front seat. Nancy pleaded with Biebighauser to take her home, promising not to tell anyone. On the way to Nancy's home, Biebighauser repeatedly apologized for what had occurred in a low voice, devoid of emotion.

As Biebighauser's car reached her home, Nancy jumped out and sprinted inside. Later that night, Nancy told her mother about the attack but didn't give all the details. She had sustained broken blood vessels in her neck, she had difficulty talking and her neck was marked and bruised. Her eye was also blackened, her face bruised.

The attack went unreported to the police.

Detectives also learned about Biebighauser's life growing up, which was equally frightening.

Daniel Roy Biebighauser was born on April 18, 1941, in St. Cloud, Minnesota, to Beverly Willcoxen and Roy Biebighauser. Biebighauser's parents were not married, and when his mother was four months pregnant, her mother contacted Roy Biebighauser's parents. The pregnancy had disgraced the Biebighauser family, and Roy's parents suggested Beverly have an abortion.

Beverly Willcoxen married Roy Biebighauser on December 15, 1940, but their life together never materialized; Beverly and Roy lived their separate lives, with Roy Biebighauser never being involved in Dan's life.

For the first two and a half years of his life, Daniel Biebighauser lived with his mother, sleeping in the same room with her until she was able to acquire an apartment with separate rooms. Around this time, Biebighauser's mother developed a relationship with a paramour. Biebighauser was then shipped off to the Willcoxen home in St. Paul, while his mother remained in Chicago.

Beverly visited her son every six weeks, sleeping with him in the same room for the weekend before returning to Chicago. When Daniel was three, she returned to St. Louis to the Willcoxen home.

When Daniel was four, he set fire to a garage, an incident that involved a fire inspector who scolded him about the incident, threatening that if it happened again, he would be placed in a foster home. It was said Daniel sat with his head down, pouting the whole time.

As Daniel aged, so did his behavioral issues. He would pout when he didn't get his way and developed a habit of stealing money and jewelry. When Beverly took up permanent living arrangements with her paramour from Chicago, this would also affect his life.

Daniel and his mother moved constantly—they lived in Paducah, Kentucky, when he was nine and then moved to Dayton, Ohio, before returning to Chicago—with the living situation always proving difficult when it came to privacy, which ultimately played a role in Daniel's jealousy toward his mother's paramour.

Daniel's mother attempted to compensate for the absence of a father figure in his life by going on picnics or fishing with him. Progressing into his teenage years, however, Daniel continued to steal, and around the age of fourteen, both he and his mother returned to his grandmother's home in St. Paul.

Around this time, a family cat owned by Daniel's uncle disappeared and was later found with its neck broken in the basement of the Willcoxen home. Since the basement was Daniel's boyhood stomping ground and there were clues he had recently gone through boxes there, Daniel was asked if he was responsible for killing the cat. He initially denied responsibility before finally admitted to doing it.

Biebighauser never gave a reason for the killing.

Daniel's bizarre behavior became sexual around the ages of sixteen and seventeen and included episodes of Daniel exposing himself to his mother as well as excessive self-gratification. Concerned, Daniel's mother reported this to his family doctor but was told it was normal for boys his age. Artwork, too, played an important part in Daniel's life.

While cleaning one day, Daniel's mother found a drawing of a nude woman folded and stuck in his dresser drawer. When confronted, he acknowledged the artwork was his. A similar occurrence was relayed by his wife, Louise, who found similar drawings, pornographic magazines and newspaper articles about a murder that occurred in Detroit in 1962.

In 1958, Beverly Biebighauser was raped and became pregnant. When she told Daniel, who was seventeen, she was met with the same indifferent, emotionless reaction others would come to know. While making preparations to come to Erie, Beverly gave Daniel two options: come to Erie or join the navy.

During his junior year of high school, Biebighauser dropped out and joined the navy. From 1959 to 1962, Biebighauser served two enlistments aboard the USS *Marias*, traveling to various countries, including the Virgin Islands, Portugal, Bermuda, Jamaica and Haiti. Biebighauser kept in contact with his mother and spent some of his leave time in Erie. It was during one of those visits that he was introduced to Louise Waibel after his mother arranged a meeting between them—shadowed, of course, by Beverly herself.

Daniel Biebighauser married Louise Waibel in October 1961. On the first night of their marriage, Daniel and his new bride traveled to Pittsburgh, accompanied by his mother and her paramour. The Biebighausers later moved to Norfolk, Virginia, while Daniel remained stationed with the navy. As far as offenses while in the military, Biebighauser's only notation consisted of a court-martial for being AWOL for eleven days. Biebighauser would receive an honorable discharge and, along with Louise and their infant son, moved back to Erie.

Although they did not admit it publicly, detectives wondered if Biebighauser was responsible for other murders and attacks.

Detective Captain Carl Kalinowski had been watching the Crotty case from the beginning and considered Biebighauser a suspect in the Mutch, Carrig and Free cases. When questioned about the murder of Eleanor Free, Biebighauser denied involvement, telling detectives that he did not know what they were talking about.

Kalinowski was determined to have state police arrive in Erie with a polygraph device as soon as possible. As for Biebighauser, he was more than willing to take a polygraph examination or be given truth serum drugs so "that once and for all they will know I am telling the truth and stop asking me questions."

On the evening of January 23, Helen Knost was brought to the Erie County Jail in an attempt to confirm whether Biebighauser was responsible for the attack on her.

Helen told District Attorney Johnson that Biebighauser was not the man who attacked her.

The true nature of the effect the murder of Lynn Crotty had on those in Erie was felt especially through the eyes and words of famed *Boston Herald* columnist George Frazier. The fifty-two-year-old Boston native, a graduate of Harvard College and recipient of the Bowdoin Prize for writing, had been passing through Erie on his way home. When he heard of the murder, Frazier decided to stick around for a few days, using Lynn Crotty's murder for his upcoming column, which would appear in the *Herald*.

Known for his impeccable style, snow-white hair and thick, black-rimmed glasses, Frazier had a tendency to haunt local nightclubs and jazz dens into the early hours of the morning. He was also known for driving his editors into a worked-up frenzy with missing deadlines. A workaholic whose prose was fueled by glasses of whiskey and chain-smoking unfiltered Camel cigarettes, Frazier seized on the similarities between the crimes Boston and Erie had been experiencing since 1963.

Both cities had experienced a rash of strangulation murders, murders forever linked to the infamous Boston Strangler. Frazier noted "an air of excitement in anticipation" of the possibility Biebighauser was Erie's Backyard Strangler. Held captive by the hazardous snowstorm that roared through the region, Frazier sat inside a restaurant next to a motor lodge on the morning of January 24 as subzero temperatures and blinding snow squalls brought Erie and its outskirts to a grinding halt.

Frazier was mesmerized by the sight outside the frost-covered windows, listening to the grinding and clicking car batteries as they stalled, with the shapes of nameless men and women struggling against the blinding snow. By eight o'clock, Frazier noted "there were 27 stalled cars, and a tow truck was making the first of what were to be hourly calls."

Frazier took the opportunity to question the public about the Lynn Crotty's murder.

"If her brothers could get at him, they'd lynch him for sure," a snowplow driver told Frazier, referring to Crotty's siblings. "Her brothers are real big boys and that strangler, why, he's no bigger'n a minute. He can't weigh more than 130 pounds soaking wet."

Frazier likened the cold, frozen Erie tundra to that of "a cheap horror movie":

> *Every so often, one of the arrivals would have his or her face swathed in bandages, for frost bite had become almost common. In downtown Erie,*

traffic was almost at a standstill and what cars were not stalled were either skidding or stuck in ruts, with neither calcium nor sodium chloride able to cut into the crusted snow that covered thick ice.

Frazier praised the writing of Tom McCormack, stating his article about his visit to Ax Murder Hollow was "a simple story of blood on the snow." The murders that occurred in Erie, claimed Frazier, portrayed Erie as "a town that never seems not touched by terror and tragedy."

Frazier's column, titled "The Quiet Ones," was written in the usual style of "pungency and elegance" he was known for. Wrapping up his experience in Erie, Frazier signed off with a question that must have been lingering in the minds of those in Erie, echoing a response to Louise Biebighauser's claim that her husband was "a quiet one": "It's always the quiet ones we must guard against, is it not?"

Biebighauser was given a polygraph examination on Friday, January 25, 1963; the test was administered by Corporal Frank Lesch of the state police. As Biebighauser was being questioned in regard to the prior attacks on women in Erie, Lynn Crotty was laid to rest; her service was held at the Church of St. Mark the Evangelist.

As Biebighauser was being questioned, the results of the tests confirmed he was telling the truth when denying involvement in the murders of Eleanor Free and Laura Mutch. Detectives confirmed this on January 27. One startling detail that was not mentioned to the press was that Biebighauser was never cleared in the sexual assault and stabbing of Clara Carrig.

The full extent of the results of Biebighauser's polygraph examination remain unknown.

The cases of Laura Mutch, Clara Carrig, Helen Knost and Eleanor Free remained unresolved. As for Daniel Roy Biebighauser, he went to trial in May that year. During closing arguments, before the case was presented to the jury, Biebighauser's defense attorney vociferously fought to ensure Biebighauser remained behind bars. "A werewolf has been walking among us," he said.

Biebighauser was soon found guilty of first-degree murder and sentenced to life imprisonment.

Life in Erie moved on, as it always did, and in 1963, an important footnote in Erie's local history occurred with the Perry sesquicentennial. The celebration spanned 120 days, from May 29 to September 10, and the city spared no expense in commemorating the 150th anniversary of the building of Oliver Hazard Perry's fleet in Erie. Those who visited Erie

Grave of Mary Lynn Crotty, Cavalry Cemetery. *Author's collection.*

Mary Lynn's casket is led from the Church of St. Mark the Evangelist. *Author's collection.*

were treated to a rededication of Perry's restored brig *Niagara*, extensive Memorial and Independence Day parades—which included everything from sailing regattas to fireworks displays—and 1813 costume–judging contests. Those who wanted to indulge themselves further in Erie's history also took part in guided historical tours or attended music and chorus festivals with their families.

On the morning of June 6, 1963, a ground-breaking ceremony was held for the new city hall, with construction expected to take up to eighteen months. The ceremony saw the arrival of many state and federal individuals for what was called "a bright new day for Downtown Erie."

Change was brewing in Erie, with the city even considering dismantling the Public Steamboat landing at Dobbins Landing.

Meanwhile, in America, a storm raged on that would forever change the country.

Across the nation, broadcast to TVs and radios in thousands of homes along the Great Lakes, racial disorder had erupted throughout the country by the time Alabama governor George Wallace stood before the entrance of the University of Alabama, protesting against integration, on June 11, 1963. President John F. Kennedy delivered his historic address on civil rights, promising a civil rights bill and asking Americans for "the kind of equality of treatment that we would want for ourselves."

On June 17, the United States Supreme Court ruled state-mandated Bible reading in schools was unconstitutional. In Erie, the Supreme Court decision was positively received by local churches and synagogues, which stated that while it was important to allow religion in schools, it was also important to protect the separation of church and state.

Locally, a joint operation between the police departments of Erie and Millcreek and the state police took place on June 22, 1963, when raids were carried out on thirty-nine locations in Erie County that were suspected of taking part in lottery and number rackets. Triggered at two o'clock in the afternoon, the raids occurred simultaneously and resulted in several arrests. Despite some locations being locked when police arrived and the evidence most likely destroyed, Detective Sergeant Weir felt the results were fruitful due to the evidence that was secured.

In a televised speech, Mayor Charles B. Williamson shared his views on civil rights, something he felt impacted Erie. Williamson's speech followed a mass rally staged by the NAACP on June 23, 1963, in Perry Square. The rally was attended by nearly one thousand people and had several speakers.

Corner of East Seventh and State Streets during the construction of Erie's new city hall, 1963. *Erie County Historical Society.*

State Street in downtown Erie, looking north, 1963. Note the "Perry sesquicentennial" signs on the lampposts. *Erie County Historical Society.*

It came at a time when Erie's local Black community was at odds with the Williamson administration's "negative attitude."

Erie experienced a water shortage, and a twenty-four-hour water ban was enacted. As June came to an end, many families sought ways to keep cool amid the rising temperatures.

On July 6, 1963, detectives for the City of Erie Police Department were handed the break they were looking for, but it came with a price.

Another woman had been attacked.

CHAPTER 8

ABDUCTION FROM THE TALLY HO

It was the afternoon of July 5, 1963, when fifty-two-year-old Davida Boyer decided to visit the Erie Public Library in search of new books to read. Boyer browsed the aisles, grabbing several books before leaving at five thirty to head back home. Walking south on State Street, Davida window shopped until she reached the southeast corner of East Eighteenth and State Streets, where she entered the Tally Ho Bar around 6:30 p.m.

A frequent customer at the bar, Davida indulged in a substantial amount of alcohol into the early morning hours of July 6. Sometime around one forty-five, Davida returned to her booth after dancing, plopping down next to her stack of library books. She settled back into her seat, the weight of the alcohol pushing against her with tremendous force.

"Come on, get out, closing!" yelled the bartender.

"I wonder who is going to walk me home tonight?" Davida said loudly, looking around.

"I will drive you home in my car," a low, soft voice responded.

She turned and saw a man with "sad eyes," wearing a brown sweater and pants. Smoke escaped from his lips as he exhaled from a cigarette, speaking politely in a "slow, lonely voice." Davida eyed a dark cap with earflaps next to an open can of beer in front of the man.

"You will? Good," Davida nodded, reaching for her library books.

The man stood up without saying a word, making his way toward the exit. Davida soon followed and exited the bar. Outside, she was greeted by the man as he stood next to an older green pickup with black siding.

Advertisement for the Tally Ho Bar. *Erie Daily Times.*

"Here it is," the man motioned, flicking his cigarette to the ground as he walked around the front and climbed into the driver's seat.

Davida was unimpressed, yet thankful for the ride home. The alcohol made her feel as if weights were attached to her feet as she crouched into the passenger seat, slamming the door shut.

The pickup sputtered to life and pulled away from the curb, turning left onto East Eighteenth Street. For Davida, the world outside felt like a blur as her face was pressed against crisp window, her eyes watching the intersection with French Street as it approached.

Davida's head twisted, her eyes trained on the intersection as the truck continued through the intersection instead of turning.

"Hey, I don't live over this way," she protested, pointing behind her. "I live up French."

"Come on," the man calmly responded. "We are going to get another drink."

"You can't get no drink at this time of the morning and I have had enough," Davida argued, her hand primed on the door handle.

The truck's engine roared as the man's foot pressed on the accelerator.

"Come on, please take me home," Davida pleaded.

Her pleas were met with silence as the truck bolted through the dark streets. Minutes later, she spotted the bay in the distance, the water glistening under the moon. The truck then came to a stop on East Front Street, overlooking the Penelec substation, humming with activity, its lights burning into the night.

The man placed the vehicle in park and turned off the ignition. He exited the truck and walked to the passenger side, jerking the door open.

Davida braced herself against the door with her left arm.

"Hey, what's going on here?" she yelled.

The man grabbed her by the arm, throwing her to the ground onto her knees. Before she could react, the man had his arm hooked around her neck. Davida's feet slid against the pavement as she struggled to fight her attacker.

Opening her mouth, Davida attempted to scream but was stifled as her attacker jammed his left hand forcefully into her throat. Her neck "burned" with pain as she wrestled back, the world around her starting to fade away. Just as she was about to black out, he removed his fingers, clutched her by her jaw and yanked out the lower plate of her false teeth.

Davida broke loose before the man attacked again, plucking her glasses from her face.

"Oh, please, sir, don't break them," Davida pleaded. "I can't see without them."

The man stood still and silent, like a predator watching his wounded prey, waiting for the final strike. He threw Davida's glasses and false teeth aside and grabbed her again, this time with his left arm. He bent her over backward and, reaching underneath her dress with his right hand, grabbed at Davida's underwear, ripping them away.

He slammed her onto the ground, diving on top of her.

"I murdered one woman for a fuck," he growled, his cheeks quivering with anger. "Now come on and put it in! I want a fuck!"

Determined, Davida broke free again, this time pushing her attacker off her. Her feet scuffed against the ground as she regained her footing, now several feet from her attacker.

"What's the matter with you?" she gasped for air.

The man's face became flushed with embarrassment, like a small child being lectured. He stuttered, stepping forward, "Come on, I want a fuck!" His voice trailed off, almost innocently. "Put it in, let's go over on the grass."

"You pig!" Davida screamed, startling her attacker. "You didn't have to ask for it like an animal! You could have asked for it like a gentleman and you might have got it!"

The man stood there dumbfounded as Davida brushed the dirt and grass from her dress.

She decided to make a run for it.

Forty-nine-year-old Sophie Gorchinsky rubbed her eyes as she looked at the clock. It was 2:25 a.m. It had been a typical night taking care of her mother, Agnes, at their home, located at 235 East Front Street. Gorchinsky heard a commotion outside and looked out the window, seeing a pickup truck kitty-corner on the street, positioned as if someone was dumping trash on the embankment. She saw a man and woman arguing next to the pickup but ignored the couple.

The commotion grew louder. Gorchinsky was about to ask the pair to leave when she heard the man speak.

"I will take you home," he pleaded. "Come on with me."

"I am not going," the woman responded defiantly, walking away into Gorchinsky's yard, out of view. The man climbed back into his pickup truck and sped away. Gorchinsky could see the woman staggering in the yard, starting to yell.

"Get me a cab! Get me a cab!" Davida Boyer screamed, while she nervously shoved a cigarette into her mouth.

Gorchinsky contacted police, but after twenty minutes, the woman disappeared.

Anne Kopes of 217 East Front Street was also awakened that night as she slept on the couch in the front room. The barking of her dog, Rex, was something that only happened when people walked up the alley or driveway. When Rex failed to stop barking, Kopes looked outside her window. Despite not seeing anything, she had the "strange feeling" that someone was standing near her tree in the front yard.

Kopes shrugged it off and went back to bed but was again awakened by her dog. Worried a prowler was outside, Kopes called out that she was going to call the cops. A few minutes passed before Kopes saw a light-colored truck go up the alley, its tires kicking up gravel as it sped away.

It was 3:09 a.m. when Officer William Serafini and his partner, Officer Willis, received a call about a possible domestic dispute on East Front Street. Responding to the scene, Serafini and Willis spotted a woman stumbling onto East Front Street after exiting a yard near German Street.

Present-day view of the location where the Tally Ho Bar used to stand on the southeast corner of State and West Eighteenth Streets. *Author's collection.*

Present-day view of East Front Street at the spot where Davida Boyer was attacked. *Author's collection.*

Serafini stopped his cruiser, rolling down the window and calling out to the woman.

Davida told the officers she had had trouble with a man and had been assaulted, losing her teeth. Serafini listened to her, noting that her stockings were disarranged and dirty and she appeared disheveled, as if some struggle had taken place. It was also clear to both officers that Davida was heavily intoxicated.

Serafini and his partner exited their cruiser and walked along the embankment where the pickup truck had been parked. In the grass, officers found Boyer's teeth, her glasses and her torn underwear. The officers also recovered a green cap with earflaps.

Detective Sergeant Thomas Stanton arrived at East Front Street at 3:20 a.m. and was greeted by both officers, who filled him in on details of the attack. Stanton was given the green men's cap and Davida Boyer's torn underwear, which were taken into evidence. Taking charge of the scene, Stanton spoke with Davida about what happened. Davida, Stanton later recalled, was highly emotional and agitated.

Stanton placed Davida into his vehicle and traveled to the Tally Ho bar, hoping he could speak with someone. However, when he arrived, Stanton found the bar locked up tight. Stanton then transported Davida to Hamot Hospital, where she was inspected for a possible rib injury and released. Arriving at headquarters, Stanton started to question Davida but realized she was too intoxicated to provide a statement and would need to be held for the day shift before providing a statement.

Davida was transported to the Erie County Jail and placed into the women's range for the night.

Officer Willis wrote up his report that morning in the presence of Officer Serafini. Not only did Davida Boyer barely escape with her life, but her attacker also claimed he previously killed a woman who refused to have sex with him. This detail did not go unnoticed.

A small clipping about the attack, which provided a brief description, appeared in the *Erie Daily Times* later that day:

> *Mrs. Boyer said the man told her he had killed one woman under similar circumstances and that he would kill another, according to her report, police said. Mrs. Boyer described the man as medium of build, about 35 years old and five feet, seven inches tall.*

Detectives realized the murder mentioned by Davida's attacker was possibly the still-unsolved murder of Laura Mutch.

The task of following up on leads in the investigation fell to Detectives Michael Snider and Charles McCurdy. The pair were well known within the detective bureau, with McCurdy referred to as the more "zealous" of the two and Snider being quieter, more reserved. "McCurdy would sometimes go off on a wild goose chase," Carl Kalinowski would remember later in life. "Mike would control McCurdy."

Snider was known for being naturally good hearted and having a soft touch. Growing up in Erie's upper east side, Snider persevered in life, developing a rapport with people on the street. He could also connect with people, something that served him well as a detective. Like others in the department, Snider was also a veteran of World War II and had been a prisoner of war for eighteen months.

McCurdy—known by his nickname, "Cubby"—was a graduate of East High School and also a World War II veteran. Together, both men went to the Tally Ho bar and spoke with the owner, Sam Campanella, and bartender Joseph LaPaglia. Campanella told detectives Davida Boyer was a regular customer and confirmed he witnessed the man she was speaking to but did not see them leave together. Campanella recommended police speak with Irene Fogle, a waitress who worked that night.

Fogle told detectives she arrived around eight o'clock on July 5 to start her shift. Davida Boyer was in the Tally Ho every night, and on the night she was attacked, she was already drinking when Fogle started her shift. The man Fogle had seen with Davida Boyer was also a customer who patronized the bar from time to time. The man, according to Fogle, wore a green cap, a brown sweater and dark pants. Fogle observed Boyer sitting with the man for much of the night and saw her drinking a substantial quantity of alcohol. Fogle remembered serving the man several draft beers, but nothing seemed out of the ordinary about his behavior.

Fogle told Snider and McCurdy she was positive she could identify the man because he had approached her several times to go out with him. As for her work at the Tally Ho bar, Fogle soon quit out of fear, and Sam Campanella barred Davida Boyer from visiting.

Detectives, on alert, took turns staking out patrons of the Tally Ho, stopping those who matched the description of Boyer's attacker. Feeling this would be their break in the Mutch investigation once a suspect was identified, police kept their next steps close to the chest.

On July 13, 1963, around nine o'clock in the evening, Irene Fogle was exiting the Celebrity Club, located at Third and State Streets, with her friend Frances Clinton. Standing outside, Fogle spotted a man in front of the Shamrock Bar. It was the same man she saw with Davida Boyer at the Tally Ho. Fogle called police headquarters and reported the sighting immediately.

Detective Sergeants Snider and McCurdy responded to the Shamrock Bar after being notified by Captain Paul J. DeDionisio that Fogle had spotted Davida Boyer's attacker, but they were unable to locate the man. The detectives spoke to Fogle, trying to gather as much information as possible about his description to locate him. Together, they entered the Shamrock, attempting to search for the man inside.

Next, the detectives visited the Wonder Bar, near Fifth and State Streets. Unable to locate the suspect there either, both detectives took a minute to plot their next move and have a drink. After several minutes, they exited onto State Street, with Fogle and Clinton trailing behind. The detectives planned to hit up Nancy's Dinor, followed by the Busy Bee.

Within minutes, they spotted a man near Nancy's Dinor who matched Fogle's description.

"That looks like him," Snider confirmed, glancing at McCurdy. Fogle nodded her head in the affirmative.

Both Snider and McCurdy rushed toward the man, presenting their badges.

"You're under arrest," Detective Snider told the man as McCurdy stepped to the other side of him. The man responded without incident.

Around nine thirty, detectives placed the suspect into a small room located off Deputy Chief Miller's office in the bureau of criminal investigation. Detectives Snider and McCurdy removed their hats and rubbers, and Detective Snider introduced himself and McCurdy to the man who sat across from them.

The man had a blank look in his eyes, his mannerisms expressionless. He spoke in a soft, slow manner, identifying himself as thirty-six-year-old John Howard Willman, a local truck driver for Benacci's Produce. Detectives began their questioning by discussing some of Willman's life and background. The highest grade he completed was eighth grade at Wilson Jr. High School, and he admitted he was able to read but was not good at writing.

Detectives confronted Willman about the attack on Davida Boyer, with McCurdy taking a chair and positioning it next to the suspect. As he sat down, McCurdy braced his arms against the back of the chair, his voice slightly raised. Willman denied being responsible for the attack and denied being at the Tally Ho Bar on the night preceding the attack.

Present-day view of the location where John Howard Willman was arrested by detectives on July 13, 1963. *Author's collection.*

Detective Snider briefly stepped out of the room and returned with Irene Fogle. Willman denied seeing Fogle and continued to deny being at the Tally Ho Bar.

Detectives asked Willman to stand up. Fogle inspected him more closely and told detectives he was the man she saw with Davida Boyer. Fogle was removed from the room before Snider continued his questioning. Willman did not budge, however, and maintained his innocence. Snider decided to then produce the cap with earflaps, presenting it to Willman.

"Does this belong to you?" Snider asked, pointing to the cap.

Willman looked on blankly.

"Yes," he responded softly.

After several more minutes, Willman confessed to assaulting Davida Boyer. Snider, having worked on the Mutch case, pushed Willman further with more questions.

"And what about the woman who was slain on Holland Street?" Snider asked.

Willman's head dropped.

"I know I did a terrible thing," he responded glumly.

Snider and McCurdy looked at each other before pressing for more information. McCurdy got up and placed a call for Captain Kalinowski and Deputy Chief Miller to come to the station. McCurdy later recollected how difficult it was to interrogate Willman, who would not provide any details about the crime.

Davida Boyer was also brought to headquarters and asked to identify if Willman was her attacker. Although she was not certain at first, Davida told detectives she recognized his eyes and his voice.

Willman, plagued with headaches, asked for aspirin, which Detective McCurdy provided.

Despite Willman confessing to murdering Laura Mutch, Detective McCurdy felt the information provided by Willman was not sufficient to take a formal statement. Detective Snider left before midnight due to personal issues, and Captain Kalinowski and Deputy Chief Miller arrived. It was decided to obtain a statement from Willman in the Boyer case.

At 11:50 p.m., Captain Kalinowski and Detective McCurdy began obtaining a statement from Willman. Kalinowski typed as he asked questions; Detective McCurdy was present as a witness. Kalinowski began the statement, asking Willman about the basics, such as his name, age and place of residence. Willman acknowledged that he was providing a statement freely and understood his statement could be used against him in a court of law.

Left: Captain Carl Kalinowski, City of Erie Police Department. *Erie Morning News*.

Right: John Howard Willman's mug shot. *Erie Daily Times*.

Kalinowski's fingers clacked against the typewriter keys.

"Now, John H. Willman, in your own words explain to me just what took place?"

> *I went to the Tally-Ho Bar at 18ᵗʰ and State Street about six-thirty PM on Friday, July 5ᵗʰ, 1963. I then started to drink beer. I was alone. After I was there a while I met a stock-car driver from Busti, New York, and we had a few beers. I then offered to buy a lady a drink. She accepted. After I bought her a drink we sat down in a booth. I then bought her some more drinks and we then danced a few times. The lady asked me for a ride home and I told her I would give her a ride home. I had the truck of my employer, The Benacci Produce Company, parked by the Tally-Ho Bar. She got in the truck and I then drove down towards the lake. We parked there and she tried to get out of the door and I pulled her back. We both fell out of the cab. Her glasses fell on top of her. The lady ran to a house, before she left she told me to get out of here. I got home some way, but I don't remember how.*

Kalinowski finished the statement by verifying that Willman was the owner of the green cap with earflaps, which Willman verbally confirmed. Willman attested his statement was the truth and that he was treated fairly and not in any way intimidated.

When Kalinowski and McCurdy finished obtaining the statement from Willman, it was 12:20 a.m. on July 14, 1963. Both men felt they finally had the break they had been searching for, a break that could also lead to other attacks and murders being connected to John Howard Willman.

All they had to do now was prove it.

CHAPTER 9

MANIAC OR DEGENERATE?

District Attorney Richard Scarpitti pulled into the driveway of 4625 Homeland Boulevard in the early morning hours of July 14, 1963, after spending a night out with his wife, Phyllis. As Scarpitti parked his vehicle, he spotted a police cruiser idling in front of his home.

Scarpitti knew something was happening.

As Scarpitti approached, the officer in the cruiser told him he needed to call the station and speak with Captain Kalinowski. Scarpitti phoned Kalinowski several minutes later and was informed that an arrest had been made in the attack on Davida Boyer. Kalinowski also told Scarpitti about Willman's admission to murdering Laura Mutch.

"Well then take him to the scene and see what he recognizes or doesn't recognize and I'll check with you," Scarpitti said.

Scarpitti told Kalinowski not to delay in bringing charges for the assault on Davida Boyer. Any statements obtained needed to be authentic and admissible, which would correlate with just how soon Willman could be charged based on the strength of the evidence.

"Make sure he's charged properly," Scarpitti cautioned.

At city hall, Willman was proving a difficult challenge for detectives.

Detective McCurdy, Deputy Chief Miller and Captain Kalinowski led Willman from Miller's office and placed him in a Detective Bureau car, with Captain Kalinowski taking the wheel. The group left city hall, traveling eastbound on East Seventh Street until they reached Parade Street, where the car turned right, proceeding south until it reached the corner of East Eighth and Parade Streets, where the vehicle stopped.

The purpose of the trip, suggested by Scarpitti, was to see if detectives could try a different angle to obtain additional information from Willman about what happened the night Laura Mutch was murdered.

Detectives asked Willman for additional details, hoping the area would jog his memory.

Willman remained silent, looking out the window.

The car sputtered forward another block, this time stopping across from Huck's Café. Here, police exited the vehicle with Willman and walked to the corner of Eighth and Parade Streets, where they turned left, walking west—along the same route they believed Laura Mutch walked before her death. They reached the corner of East Eighth and Holland Streets, under the towering brick building.

Willman remained silent, shuffling along with the detectives, and the "field trip" failed to yield any new clues. Soon, the men walked back to the car and returned to city hall between two thirty and three o'clock in the morning. Willman was again questioned for about an hour before he was placed in a cell for the night, and an exhausted Detective McCurdy headed home.

When Willman was brought in for questioning, detectives searched records within the department for possible prior records. At first, nothing indicated Willman had been involved in any major crimes, and he had never been photographed or fingerprinted. Willman was, however, arrested for minor incidents in 1956 and 1958.

On July 29, 1958, Willman, then thirty-one, was arrested with Julia Bird Hall and Fred Alvin Hall by Detective Lewis Penman of the state police. The three had been involved in a thieving scheme on Presque Isle Park on July 25, 1958. The scheme consisted of Julia Bird Hall walking along the beach, a towel in hand. Dropping the towel over an unattended purse, Hall walked away, holding the purse concealed by the towel. The theft did not go unnoticed, and almost immediately, the purse's owner, Elina Clark, followed Hall and wrote down the license plate of Hall's vehicle before it left. She then contacted police, who arrested the three the following day.

Fred and Julia Hall pleaded guilty to larceny, with Willman admitting to transporting them to the scene. The purse, according to the Halls, was later buried in the sand after they discovered no money was inside. All three were jailed in lieu of $500 bail each. Willman was indicted for larceny and being an accessory after the fact and on September 4, 1958, was sent to the Erie County Prison and fined $100. Fred Alvin Hall was sentenced to the Western Penitentiary for three to six years and Julia Bird Hall to the Women's Prison in Muncy for an indefinite term.

Kalinowski believed Willman, who was a boarder in the Hall home on Buffalo Road, was easily coaxed into the thievery scheme. The evidence suggested that the Halls took advantage of Willman because of his mental deficiency. It was the arrest that occurred on December 16, 1956, for disorderly conduct in Lawrence Park that made Kalinowski's stomach churn.

After Willman was placed his cell, Kalinowski drove out to the Lawrence Park Police Department, where he spoke with Sergeant Strong. Kalinowski provided Strong with an update about Willman's arrest and subsequent confession in the Laura Mutch case. Curiosity and concern caused Kalinowski to question Strong about the 1956 arrest and whether he remembered the incident.

"Yes, I remember the incident very well," Sergeant Strong replied, an odd look washing over his face. "I was on patrol in the park late one afternoon, just before Christmas, when I came across this fellow. He was sitting in a parked car in a secluded area near a children's playground. On the seat next to him were a pair of trousers, and a pair of women's panties and other lingerie. After I took him in for questioning, we discovered that he was wearing women's underwear beneath his own work clothes."

Strong told Kalinowski that Willman's clothes consisted of a dirty sweatshirt, shoes, socks and the ladies' underwear he was wearing.

"Did he tell you what he was doing there in the park?" Kalinowski asked.

"Well," Strong said, hesitating briefly. "You might say he was behaving unnaturally. Later, when we took him before Justice of the Peace John Nuss, he pleaded guilty to disorderly conduct and was fined $19."

Kalinowski nodded, wiping his eyes with exhaustion. He decided to head home.

He had a feeling it was going to be a long day.

Later that day, around 1:20 p.m., Detective McCurdy arrived at headquarters. Still bothered by a lack of sufficient information connected to Willman's confession to the murder of Laura Mutch, McCurdy asked Detectives Herman Nowak and Melvin Swanson if they would question Willman alone.

Melvin and Nowak questioned Willman, which took about an hour. Detective McCurdy then questioned Willman around three o'clock, lasting about an hour and a half. Much to McCurdy's frustration, Willman was still not providing any details. Temporarily pushing his frustration aside, McCurdy and Detective Swanson transported Willman to the home of Alderman Michael J. Kinecki for his arraignment in the attack on Davida Boyer.

The home of Harry and Catherine Willman, 452 East Eighth Street. *Author's collection.*

The warrant was presented to Alderman Kinecki, and John Willman was formerly charged by Detective McCurdy with assault with intent to ravish. McCurdy obtained a notarization for Willman's statement in the Boyer attack and a search warrant for 452 East Eighth Street, the home of Catherine and Harry Willman, John's brother and sister-in-law, to search for Davida Boyer's missing library books.

Willman entered a plea of guilty.

Prior to Willman's arraignment, on the direction of District Attorney Scarpitti, Kinecki ordered Willman held and his bail set at $5,000, which would keep Willman behind bars while detectives worked on his connection to the Laura Mutch case. Following the arraignment, Willman was returned to the city jail, and McCurdy and Swanson drove to 452 East Eighth Street to serve the warrant.

Detectives McCurdy and Swanson introduced themselves to John's brother, Harry, and his wife, Catherine, telling them they wanted to talk about John and informing them he'd been picked up in relation to an assault charge. Harry and Catherine Willman allowed detectives inside and gave them permission to search John's possessions. The detectives asked if John had recently brought home library books or any women's panties.

Both Harry and Catherine answered in the negative.

While staying with his brother and sister-in-law, John Willman slept on a couch in a rear room of the home, which held only a few dressers, meaning John's personal items were few. Within twenty minutes, McCurdy and Swanson finished their search, leaving empty-handed. On their way back to city hall, both men decided to stop for a much-needed bite to eat and some coffee.

It was eight o'clock that evening when McCurdy and Swanson attempted to question John Willman again.

Two hours later, McCurdy found himself in familiar territory as he tousled his hair in frustration and stood up in a haze of cigarette smoke before exiting the conference room.

"I'll be back." McCurdy told Swanson, slamming the door behind him.

Fifty-one-year-old Paul J. DeDionisio was tall, with jet-black hair and a prominent nose. His good looks and attitude descended from a well-known and respected Italian family in the city of Erie. As the captain sat in his office at the front of the department, he heard a knock on his door.

DeDionisio glanced up from some paperwork as McCurdy entered.

"Captain, could you please come back and talk to this fellow a little while?" McCurdy asked, frustrated. "I'd like to have you talk to him to see how you can make out with him."

DeDionisio told McCurdy he'd be happy to assist, and both men walked back to the conference room. DeDionisio entered and introduced himself to Willman, still seated at the table.

"Well," McCurdy motioned to the door, "we'll stay outside and we'll stand by the door there and this way you can talk to him alone and maybe he might tell you something that he didn't tell us."

"All right, fine." DeDionisio responded as both detectives left, closing the door.

DeDionisio flashed a welcoming smile to Willman, tugging gently at his tie.

"What's your name?" DeDionisio asked.

"John Willman."

"Well, John, I understand that you are confessing to making remarks, that you are confessing to a murder," DeDionisio responded, sitting down across from him. "Now, before I even ask you any questions of anything, I want you to know this: You don't have to tell me anything. You don't have to answer, you don't have to talk to me if you don't want to. The only thing I'm back here for is to talk to you. If you want to tell me the truth that's what I'm here for, to seek out the truth. Now if you want to talk to me, if you want to tell me, fine. But I repeat again, you don't have to talk to me."

Willman stared back in silence.

"Well, now this woman in question that you was supposed to have killed, what was her name?"

"Mrs. Mutch," Willman mumbled.

"Well," DeDionisio started. "Now, you know, before you start to talk to me, and you start to telling me that you killed some woman, I want you to know how serious this is. This is a very serious charge. You know in Pennsylvania, in the Commonwealth of Pennsylvania you could go to the electric chair if you're found guilty, you could get a life sentence, and you could probably go for a number of years, maybe."

Willman again remained silent before DeDionisio's booming voice continued. "Now, don't tell me that you killed this woman if you didn't kill her. All I'm interested in is the truth."

Willman's mouth quivered and eyes flickered, his stare bouncing back and forth between DeDionisio and the table.

DeDionisio knew getting answers was going to be difficult.

"Look, John," DeDionisio continued. "I don't want to be putting words in your mouth, or I don't want to be leading you on. I don't want to be telling you. You tell me what you done."

Willman nodded, his gaze connecting with DeDionisio.

"Well, I was up to the café. I believe they call it Huck's on Parade Street. I had a few drinks and I was going home. I was on my way home and a woman passed me. She was going in the opposite direction." Willman paused, taking the time to remember. "Then I turned around and I commenced to follow her. I caught up to her and I started to talk to her. I asked her 'Aren't you afraid to walk alone?' and she said, 'Yes.'"

DeDionisio looked on as the words trickled out of Willman.

"She was talking about religion. That's all she would talk about. Just talk about religion and she was carrying a Bible," Willman continued. "Then we continued walking and then we walked between two houses, two buildings, we walked between two buildings and when we were in the back she slipped and fell on the ice. Then, I got down on her and I grabbed her and I pulled her scarf around her neck, shoved her dress up, pulled her pants off, and I screwed her."

Willman paused, his mouth askew as he searched for what to say next.

"And then, I left."

DeDionisio leaned in.

"John, look, I'm going to repeat myself. I want you to understand. This is a very, very serious charge, and like I explained to you before, you know

Former location of Huck's Café on Parade Street. *Author's collection.*

that if this case would ever get to a Court of Law before a jury and if you were found guilty, in the Commonwealth of Pennsylvania you could get the electric chair. You could get life imprisonment for life or maybe a number of years. Now, don't tell me that you committed this murder, that you killed this woman if you didn't do it."

"No." Willman shook his head before nodding. "I done it. I know, it was a terrible thing. I want to get it off my mind. It's been bothering me."

"Now is that why you're confessing to this?" DeDionisio asked. "Did somebody tell you to confess to this? Why are you confessing to this? Why are you telling me this?"

"Because, it bothered me. I know I done a terrible thing."

"John, did you listen to television or radio or read the newspapers?"

"Yes."

"You know about the Eleanor Free case? Do you remember that?" DeDionisio asked. "Hey, you killed her too, didn't you?"

"Oh, no," Willman responded, his eyes widened with surprise. "No, I didn't."

"Why, you told me a little while ago that you did," DeDionisio continued, testing Willman's reaction.

"No, I didn't tell you that. I didn't kill anybody else."

"Are you sure of that?"

"Yes." Willman nodded his head. "I'm sure."

"Alright," DeDionisio responded as he stood up.

Opening the door, he looked out to McCurdy and Swanson. "Come on in the office here. I want you to listen to what John Willman has to say."

Both detectives entered, and Captain DeDionisio closed the door behind them. The detectives looked on as DeDionisio turned his attention back to Willman.

"Now, John, before you start telling this story again like you told me, before you tell it to these men here—now you know who they are because they have been talking to you. Don't tell this story if it's not true."

Willman continued, repeating the story he told Captain DeDionisio, almost word for word. DeDionisio stood back, his arms folded, with growing curiosity.

"Hey, John, how did you kill this woman?"

"Well," Willman responded, looking blankly at the detectives. "She had a scarf on her and I pulled that scarf real tight and I choked her and I shoved it in her mouth."

"Let's see how." DeDionisio continued, to the surprise of McCurdy and Swanson.

"Do you have a handkerchief?" Willman asked.

DeDionisio pulled a handkerchief from his pocket, handing it to Willman. The handkerchief proved to be too small, and detectives were left looking for something comparable for Willman's demonstration. In the corner of the room, they located a black satchel with a towel inside.

"John, take this towel," DeDionisio said, handing it to Willman. "And you show me how, what you done with this scarf."

Willman took the towel and started to tie it around his neck but stopped, saying the towel was not long enough to wrap around behind him. After several attempts, Willman brought the towel up and behind his neck. He then tied the knot, shoving the rest of the towel into his mouth.

DeDionisio looked to the detectives, satisfied Willman's statement was accurate.

"Well, look, fellows," DeDionisio said. "I'm going to go back up to the front office again. If this man here is willing to give you a voluntary statement, go ahead and take it."

Captain DeDionisio returned to his office.

It was eleven thirty when Detective McCurdy began typing the statement of John Willman in relation to the murder of Laura Mutch, while Detective Swanson remained as a witness. Both detectives finished the statement

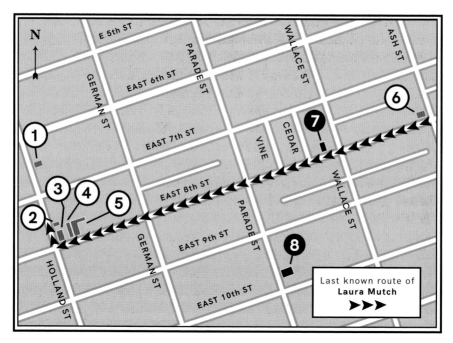

(1) Mutch home, (2) 717 Holland Street, (3) Muffler King building, (4) Hill Mill Dairy, (5) Scobell Manufacturing, (6) Gospel Tabernacle Church, (7) Willman home and (8) Huck's Café.

an hour later, during the morning of July 15, 1963. Detectives also asked Willman about the murder of Eleanor Free and a murder that was fabricated to scrutinize Willman's responses.

Willman denied both and was returned to his cell.

Later that morning, before noon, District Attorney Scarpitti visited the police department. After being briefed by Captain Kalinowski on the investigation, Scarpitti entered Deputy Chief Miller's office and was briefed by Deputy Chief Miller and Safety Director Hetico. After reading Willman's typed statement, Scarpitti wanted an opportunity to speak with Willman in person, with Kalinowski acting as a witness. Willman was brought into the conference room, and Scarpitti confronted him with his confession.

Scarpitti analyzed fragments of the statement, asking if Willman had been to Huck's Café. His questions were also focused on gauging Willman's response to a description of Laura Mutch's Bible. Captain Kalinowski also interjected with questions of his own, asking Willman if he heard any dogs barking when he killed Laura Mutch.

Willman's responses to these questions were consistent, his words kept at a minimum; he only nodded his head in the affirmative, responding, "Uh huh."

After speaking with Willman, Scarpitti remained skeptical of his involvement in the murder. Although Willman did not outright deny his involvement, Scarpitti honed in on the accuracy of Willman's statement, which was not supported by any evidence. After speaking with Deputy Chief Miller, Kalinowski and others, Scarpitti recommended Willman be examined by a psychiatrist.

That evening, John's brothers, Harry and Eugene, and their wives, Catherine and Carol, went to the police department to try to visit John. When approaching the front desk, John's siblings asked if they could see him. The officer behind the desk told them no, ignoring further questions, which included an attempt to pass along a pack of cigarettes for John.

"Make an appointment with Mr. Miller to come see him, when you come see Mr. Miller," the officer said curtly, turning his attention to paperwork before him. Deputy Chief Miller, the officer said, was not available.

Unable to make any progress, John's siblings and sisters-in-law left, planning to follow up the next morning. After Willman's family left, around seven o'clock in the evening, Captain DeDionisio went to the cell range and, using a pair of keys, opened Willman's cell door.

"How are you today, John?"

"Aw, pretty good," Willman responded.

"Are you getting a lot of rest?"

"Yeah," Willman said. "I'm getting a lot of sleep. I'm getting a lot of rest."

"All right," DeDionisio said, stepping aside. "Come on, John, I'll exercise you a bit."

For the next thirty minutes, DeDionisio walked up and down the hallway with Willman, giving him an opportunity to stretch his legs. DeDionisio also used the chance to question to Willman more.

"John, you know the last time I talked to you, you told me that you killed this woman," DeDionisio said, stopping in the hallway. "I want to repeat myself. Like I told you before, John, this is a very serious thing and I want you to realize that."

Willman stood there, listening.

"Now, I don't want you to confess to this murder if you didn't do it. Are you making this up?"

"No," Willman responded, shaking his head. "I'm not making it up. I know, I know I done a terrible thing."

"Well, all right. But I want you to be sure," DeDionisio responded, before heading back downstairs. Approaching the turnkey, he motioned for Willman to follow.

ERIE'S BACKYARD STRANGLER

"John, come on," DeDionisio said, turning to Willman. "We'll get a little breath of fresh air outside."

The men exited city hall on the northern side of the sidewalk, next to a pair of large steps leading to the entrance. DeDionisio handed Willman a cigarette, which he readily accepted, stuffing it into his mouth as he and DeDionisio made small talk, commenting on the weather and talking about his background and family. Minutes later, DeDionisio led Willman back inside to his cell.

The following day, July 16, 1963, Carol and Katherine Willman and Harry Willman spoke to Deputy Chief Miller while bringing John extra pairs of clothing. The Willmans again asked to see him and were denied access, with Miller reasoning that John wanted no visitors and they would need to wait until John was transferred to the county jail before visitations were granted.

When asked about Willman's bond, Miller informed them that the bond was $500, cautioning them not to bond him out because it was easier for the police to keep him incarcerated rather than chase after him for appointments and medical examinations with the psychiatrist. Willman's siblings informed Miller that they did not have the money to bond him out and, when discussing an attorney, were told by Miller that an attorney would be provided for John when he needed to have one, as long as he could prove he was indigent.

That evening, around six o'clock, Willman was transferred to the Erie County Prison, located behind the county courthouse on West Sixth Street.

For five days, Willman had not had access to relatives, had not retained an attorney and had had no attorney to advise him of his constitutional rights.

When Willman was transferred to the county prison, Dr. Frank Pizzat, a clinical psychologist, was asked to perform several examinations at the request of the district attorney's office. In his meeting with Willman, Pizzat utilized a variety of tests, such as the Wexler-Bellevue Intelligence Scale, Rorschach inkblot tests, the Thematic Apperception Test and the Bender-Gestalt Test, which utilizes human figure drawing.

Through additional examinations, performed over the next several weeks, Dr. Pizzat determined Willman was considered "mild mentally defective," with a reported IQ of sixty-three. In analyzing some of the results, Dr. Pizzat concluded that Willman's typical reactions to problems surrounding abstract thinking scored a zero, the reason being that Willman could not solve any of them.

According to Dr. Pizzat, the results of the Wexler-Bellevue examination indicated that Willman was "mentally retarded." Despite learning about Willman's personality and mental capabilities, Pizzat was unable to state with any high level of confidence whether Willman was involved in Laura Mutch's murder.

In attempting to explain how Willman thought, responded and acted, Pizzat would later state that Willman "is incapable of reasoning in the abstract sense of the word."

While Willman was incarcerated at the county prison, detectives dug further into his life and background. After dropping out of school in the eighth grade, he joined the national guard, serving several months overseas in Germany, where he was stationed. On returning home, Willman worked at General Electric briefly before being laid off. By now, Willman was able to accept visits from his family, but he still had no counsel advising him in regard to his case or his legal rights.

As the days dragged on, Willman's family began to suspect something else was going on. One of the days Detective McCurdy visited Catherine Willman at her home, she asked McCurdy why her brother-in-law was left at the city jail for so many days without being transferred to the county courthouse on just a single charge of assault.

"It must be something more," she pressed, trying to get a response from McCurdy.

McCurdy finally admitted that John was a suspect in the murder of Laura Mutch. Sharing this with Willman's family allowed McCurdy, in turn, to learn more details about John's life, including his behavior in both public and private. John's brother, Harry, was also informed of John's involvement as a suspect in the Mutch murder.

Detective McCurdy told the Willmans it would be in their best interest not to tell anyone about John being held for the Mutch murder, because it might harm him when the time came for trial. Harry and Catherine Willman told McCurdy that they would remain silent.

As for McCurdy and the other detectives, their investigation turned up few clues. Willman claimed that on the night of December 30, 1960, he had been drinking at Huck's Café and, while walking home, encountered Laura Mutch as she was on her way home from church.

Harry Willman told detectives that this would have been impossible. His brother had gone to bed early that night, which was not out of the ordinary. Harry's other brother and sister-in-law and their children were also over. Willman's bedroom, located in the back of the home, had windows that were nailed shut and covered with plastic during the winter months.

If John Willman were to have left that night, he would have had to open the windows forcefully, leaving evidence of damage to the windows, or he would have had to exit by walking through the house in view of his family.

There was no evidence, according to Harry Willman, of either scenario.

Detectives also questioned Michael DeSantis Jr., the bartender at Huck's Café. DeSantis could not remember seeing Willman, a regular customer, on the night of the murder. Despite detectives telling Willman hair was found at the scene that implicated him, which was untrue, there was no physical evidence linking him to the backyard of 717 Holland Street.

On August 30, 1963, Detective McCurdy visited Willman in prison and escorted him to the courthouse for a polygraph examination. Later that day, at the Marine Bank building downtown, District Attorney Scarpitti met with Detectives McCurdy and Snider, recommending another statement to determine whether Willman had changed his mind about confessing to the murder and if any further details were gleamed from Willman about what happened. With this second confession, Scarpitti hoped to clear up concerns that lingered following the first confession.

The following day, McCurdy and Snider went to the county prison with a plan to interrogate Willman and obtain a second statement. During this interrogation, McCurdy asked the questions.

Several weeks passed as the district attorney's office mulled over the evidence and mental examinations. On the morning of September 26, 1963, District Attorney Scarpitti held a conference in his office with detectives to reexamine the evidence and statements. After some consideration, Scarpitti decided to bring a charge of murder against John Howard Willman for the killing of Laura Mutch.

At 11:15 a.m., in a joint statement released to the press, District Attorney Scarpitti and Deputy Chief Miller informed the press that Detective Sergeant Charles McCurdy had been instructed to file murder charges against Willman before Alderman Kinecki.

"This arrest is the culmination of a careful investigation by the city Bureau of Criminal Investigation in cooperation with the District Attorney's office," the statement read. "Because of the assistance of the fifty-two-year-old woman, who furnished original information and by virtue of competent interrogation by the detective bureau this case was solved, and we know Erie residents will rest somewhat easier tonight."

Willman was arraigned before Alderman Kinecki around 12:35 p.m. At Willman's arraignment, he entered a plea of not guilty and was remanded to the county jail without bail. Because Willman was considered indigent, court-appointed counsel was provided. District Attorney Scarpitti started to prepare for the preliminary hearing, scheduled for October 4, 1963, with the possibility of trial occurring during the November term of court.

Information about Willman, the confessions and the assault on Davida Boyer slowly leaked to the public. What the public also learned was that Willman had been held for almost two months before being charged with the murder.

District Attorney Scarpitti proudly proclaimed that Willman was "the best suspect we ever had in the Mutch case."

The following morning, in two separate interviews that spanned a total of two hours, Willman was questioned by a reporter from the *Erie Morning News*.

"She told me to go to church and get religion, that's all I remember," Willman said, speaking in "halting monotones." "They said I confessed I killed her. I don't really remember much."

Willman fidgeted nervously while he spoke. "They talked to me for five days at the police station. I had splitting headaches. I signed a statement but I don't know anything about killing any woman," Willman mumbled. "I just want to go home."

Willman spoke about the challenges he'd faced in his life, including leaving school at an early age due to his mental difficulties and dealing with the death of his parents at a young age. Even as he spoke about his life, Willman failed to expand on his responses, leaving much to be desired.

John Howard Willman is photographed leaving the Erie County Jail for his arraignment on September 26, 1963. *Erie Morning News*.

Willman denied having anything against women and said he was sorry about the murder of Laura Mutch. "I'm sorry she's dead and I'm sorry for where it has put me."

When asked about Davida Boyer, Willman claimed to know nothing about the assault, saying he didn't remember.

The celebration of Willman's arrest was short-lived. Later that night, the Reverend Dr. Lewis Hillyard, local ACLU president, criticized the district attorney's office and its handling of Willman's case and confession. "The long period of confinement of the defendant without legal counsel and the apparent punitive $5,000 bond set on the attempted assault charge strike me as unusual," Hillyard commented to the *Erie Daily Times*.

The condemnation forced Scarpitti to play defense. "The court does not provide counsel for indigents until the defendant is

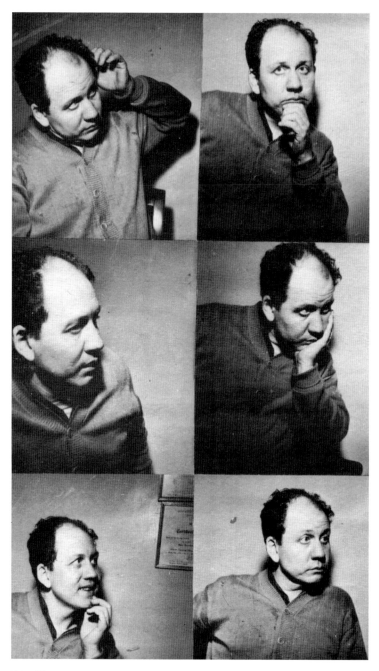

John Howard Willman is photographed in the Erie County Jail while being interviewed by a reporter for the *Erie Morning News*. *Author's collection.*

called before the bench to plead guilty or innocent and asks for counsel to defend himself," he responded. "The investigation was actually concluded the morning the announcement of [the] murder charge against Willman was made on the final checkout of the fact that the defendant was on public assistance rolls on Dec. 30, 1960, which therefore ruled out any work alibi. I had no other choice but to file the charge on the strength of the suspect's purported confession of the Mutch murder to city detectives. I have to keep him in jail on the strength of the confession."

When asked why Willman had such an abnormally high bond, Scarpitti said releasing Willman would "have been taking a chance he would have committed a crime while being investigated. So I set the bond at $5,000 to guarantee he would stay in jail."

The same day the ACLU entered the case, Erie County judge Elmer L. Evans appointed attorneys James E. Beveridge and Bernard F. Quinn to handle Willman's defense.

James E. Beveridge, a graduate of East High School in 1950, graduated from Gannon College in 1954 and later received his law degree from the University of Pennsylvania in 1959. Beveridge was also a former first lieutenant in the U.S. Army.

Forty-five-year-old Bernard F. Quinn, a native of Dushore, Pennsylvania, was raised in Erie and was a graduate of Cathedral Preparatory School. Quinn obtained his undergraduate degree at Holy Cross College and was attending Harvard Law School when, in 1941, during World War II, he enlisted in the U.S. Army. Following the war, Quinn received his law degree from Dickinson School of Law and returned to Erie.

On Saturday, September 28, 1963, Lawrence Park sergeant Edward Strong identified Willman as the man he arrested in 1956. Captain DeDionisio echoed concerns about Willman's criminal past, instructing any police departments to contact detectives in Erie if they had had prior run-ins with Willman. While the shocked public learned more about Willman, Scarpitti continued to deny his office did anything wrong by holding Willman without counsel, "This man was not deprived of counsel," Scarpitti said, "and he could have had it any time he wanted."

Following his appointment as Willman's attorney, Quinn indicated that he and Beveridge would petition the court for a continuance of the preliminary hearing for at least a few weeks and that he would convey these thoughts to the district attorney to see if he would be agreeable.

Erie Daily Times columnist Ed Matthews echoed a sentiment many locals resonated with: "The suspect could be the killer but the time is the issue."

Bernard F. Quinn and James E. Beveridge, court-appointed defense attorneys for John Howard Willman. *Erie Morning News.*

On September 30, the ACLU announced plans to have a lawyer represent the organization at Willman's preliminary hearing. "As far as the ACLU can determine," attorney Roger E. Fischer, vice president of the ACLU, said, "Willman should have been given counsel Sept. 3 when he was brought to the Erie County Court for the call of the list for the September term of criminal court."

Fischer pointed out that Willman, then charged with the assault of Davida Boyer, was brought in with several other defendants. All of these defendants were asked how they wished to plead and whether they wished to have an attorney. "Willman was not asked, and it was later determined his case had been continued."

Fischer's statements drew criticism from former district attorney Herbert J. Johnson Jr., now an Orphans Court judge, who handled the call of the list for the September term. Johnson confirmed that the fact that Willman was not asked did not violate his constitutional rights. "Counsel is appointed only when a plea is taken from the defendant, and then only at his request," Johnson concluded.

From the beginning, attorneys Quinn and Beveridge hit the ground running in preparing Willman's defense. They reached out to witnesses, dissected Willman's confession and reviewed Dr. Pizzat's psychiatric examinations.

On October 2, 1963, Davida Boyer spoke to a reporter from the *Erie Morning News*, telling her story of the attack. Davida, held in the Erie County Jail for attempting to defraud a taxi driver, provided details that differed from when she first spoke to police and her future testimony at Willman's trial.

"We got into his truck and I must have fallen asleep because the next thing I knew I sat up in the truck and saw bay water," Boyer told the reporter. "It was then that he stopped the truck, ran around to my side of the cab and pulled me out. His fingers were in my mouth and he choked me until things started going black. I prayed and all of a sudden he took his hand away from my mouth. He took off my glasses just as gentle as an eye doctor and laid them in the grass. Then he picked me up and threw me into some gravel. He told me he killed one woman and he'd kill me too if he had to."

Two local doctors interviewed for the article, a pathologist and a urologist, were asked if Willman, as described by Davida, could have been responsible for the murder of Laura Mutch, based on the evidence provided. Both strongly indicated their doubt that he was responsible for Mutch's murder, saying, "Certain psychic conditions could produce different effects in a man on the two nights in question."

After speaking with attorneys Beveridge and Quinn, District Attorney Scarpitti announced he would not oppose a request for a continuation. Scarpitti did confirm, however, that Willman's confession would be made public at the preliminary hearing.

Because no court stenographer was available to record the preliminary hearing, a temporary postponement moved the hearing to October 7, 1963, at the office of Alderman Kinecki. In Quinn and Beveridge's meeting with Willman prior to the hearing, they encountered nothing but blank responses while struggling to discuss the case, prompting endless frustration. The ACLU continued to monitor the case, announcing that local attorney John M. Wolford would be retained to act as an observer at the hearing to ensure Willman's constitutional rights had not been, nor would be, violated.

Wolford, a native of Corry, Pennsylvania, was a graduate of Strong Vincent High School. He graduated from Yale University and obtained his law degree from University of Pennsylvania Law School. Wolford was also a veteran of World War II, having served with the U.S. Navy. Since 1957, he had been a partner in the firm of Dunn and Wolford.

Willman appeared with his attorneys before Alderman Kinecki on the afternoon of October 7, 1963, to determine if the district attorney's office had sufficient evidence to have Willman bound over for charges. Scarpitti made it no secret that Willman's confessions were the key to the prosecution's case. As for attorneys Beveridge and Quinn, the plan for the defense was to invalidate the confessions with their own expert witnesses, relying heavily on statements from Davida Boyer.

Those present were surprised when Willman pleaded not guilty and, on the advice of his attorneys, waived his right to a preliminary hearing, setting the stage for the trial to be presented before the grand jury on October 28. This move by the defense, which confused many, led Willman's attorneys to declare that the preliminary hearing was not a determination of guilt or innocence.

Willman's attorneys felt that proceeding with the hearing would only "harass" their client without their being able to provide a defense, something Beveridge and Quinn stated they could do at a trial before a jury. Willman's waiving of the preliminary hearing, although it did not limit his defense, did reduce his attorneys' ability to file a motion for habeas corpus, known as a motion to quash.

"The court appointed us to protect the rights of John Willman and that is all we're interested in," Beveridge and Quinn told reporters. "We feel these rights will be better protected by not going into the hearing."

As both sides prepared for the grand jury, the public dispute between the district attorney and ACLU continued to escalate. On October 9, District Attorney Scarpitti challenged the Erie chapter of the ACLU to make its findings public.

"The preliminary hearing is over now," Scarpitti said. "If the ACLU believes any civil liberties have been violated, now is the time for them to make public their findings, or present a petition to the county court, asking for a writ of habeas corpus."

Attorney Wolford, who attended the preliminary hearing, told the *Erie Daily Times* he would present his opinion within the next day or so.

"I know no rights were violated, the deputy attorney general says they were not, and the courts will say they were not," Scarpitti said. "It's up to the ACLU now."

The following morning, the Reverend Dr. Lewis Hillyard, pastor of the First Unitarian Church and local president of the ACLU, issued a scathing reply. "The district attorney is well aware that the ACLU is more concerned with the preservation and protection of the civil liberties of a defendant than in making headlines. He should also be aware that were we to prematurely release the results of our inquiry, we would not only be risking the possibility of infringing upon the effective representation of the accused's legal defenses, but would also be guilty of the very practice of 'Trial by Publicity' which we deplore," Hillyard's statement said. "This organization has repeatedly emphasized that it is concerned with the defendant's Constitutional rights, not with the question of his guilt or innocence."

Attorney Wolford also released a statement:

> *Our investigation and review of recent Supreme Court decisions has convinced myself John H. Willman's constitutional rights were violated through the failure to have counsel at either of the two arraignments, both of which are for serious felonies, by his long incarceration without benefit of counsel, by the continuance of the assault charge without the defendant's knowledge or concern, and perhaps others.*
>
> *However, as an observer only, I am fully convinced that, irrespective of the quantum of experience in criminal court, Bernard F. Quinn, Esq., and James E. Beveridge, Esq., are highly competent counsel, are fully cognizant of the constitutional problems, and more than equal to their responsibility. The choice of approach to the problems must and will be left to their capable hands.*
>
> *It is not my wish or desire personally, or the function of the American Civil Liberties Union to enter into a political controversy in which neither I nor the Union are a part, particularly since its prolongation seems to daily prejudice the rights of the defendant further, irrespective of his guilt or innocence.*

On November 1, 1963, the grand jury returned an indictment against Willman for the murder of Laura Mutch. That morning, defense attorneys filed a motion to quash the indictment on the grounds that television and radio publicity of the indictment Thursday night would be detrimental to a fair and impartial trial. In response, Judge Samuel Y. Rossiter set no hearing date for the motion, but legal experts presumed that it would be heard before the trial on November 18.

Despite grand jury findings not officially being revealed until the morning of November 1, the *Erie Daily Times* was aware of the indictment having been returned since twelve thirty in the afternoon on the day prior, when a reporter, Garth Minegar, stood in the courthouse hallway as grand jury witnesses were told they would need to return on November 18. Avoiding a possible scandal, in addition to the public squabble between the ACLU and the district attorney's office, staff of the *Times* and *Erie Morning News* withheld their scoop until the official ruling was announced, a move that earned the papers wide praise. Although the newspapers delayed releasing information, news of the indictment was prematurely released on the night of October 31 by WJET radio and WICU-TV.

Judge Rossiter granted Willman's attorneys a rule to show cause on their motion to quash the indictment on November 9, 1963, which postponed Willman's trial until February the following year. Meanwhile, a hearing was set for December 17 to address the motion to throw out Willman's indictment.

On December 10, 1963, Willman's attorneys motioned to petition the court to suppress Willman's confessions made during his initial detention from July 14 to September 27. Willman's attorneys also petitioned to order the district attorney to divulge particular items of evidence the prosecution planned to use at trial.

On December 17, 1963, Judge Burton R. Laub oversaw testimony from four newspapermen and the foreman of the November grand jury in relation to the premature leak of Willman's indictment. Hyle Vance Richmond, a reporter for WICU-TV and radio, testified he became aware of the indictment sometime after four o'clock in the afternoon on October 31. When pressed about the source he received the information from over the phone, Richmond declined to confirm who provided the information to him.

Erie Morning News reporter Tom McCormack testified he was aware of radio stations reporting on the air that an indictment had been returned against Willman. McCormack said he found no evidence that an indictment had been released and attempted to reach out to both the prosecution and the defense attorneys for verification. McCormack also testified that he spoke to Garth Minegar, court reporter for the *Times*, who told him he had reason to believe an indictment had been returned.

John Dunn, a reporter for WJET, testified he received information similar to that obtained by Hyle Vance Richmond from WICU. Dunn, too, declined to reveal his source. Garth Minegar, the last newspaperman to testify, revealed he overheard remarks that an indictment had been returned against Willman while standing in the hallway at the courthouse. Minegar revealed that he overheard District Attorney Scarpitti speaking to County Detective George Wochner and that, based on their discussion, Minegar

Downtown Erie, State Street looking south between Sixth and Seventh Streets. *Erie County Historical Society.*

understood that an indictment had been returned and witnesses would be called back on November 18 for trial.

Minegar continued his testimony, stating that he chose to withhold this information before the official findings were released. During oral arguments, Judge Laub stated that an indictment is merely a formal accusation and that the secrecy around grand jury proceedings is designed to protect jurors from intimidation. Willman's attorneys disputed this, saying the proceedings should have remained a secret until returned in open court or before a judge.

With 1963 coming to an end, district attorney–elect Edward Carney met with members of the district attorney's staff on December 20, 1963, for briefings on Willman's upcoming trial. Prior to his meeting, Carney had advised two attorneys he planned to select as assistant district attorneys, Robert J. Kelleher and Michael M. Palmisano, to attend the trial that addressed Willman's indictment.

Born in 1913 in Erie, Edward H. Carney was a well-known, lifelong resident of the city. A graduate of Strong Vincent High School, Carney attended Allegheny College and the University of Pittsburgh Law School.

Carney returned to Erie, where he practiced law until the outbreak of World War II, when he became an FBI agent. Following the war, Carney returned home and continued practicing law. Prior to winning the 1963 election for district attorney, Carney was a state special deputy attorney general from 1960 to 1962 and served as counsel for the Fraternal Order of Police Haas Memorial Lodge and the Erie Fraternal Order of Police.

On December 23, 1963, Judge Burton R. Laub upheld Willman's indictment, clearing the way for the case to head to trial.

On January 9, 1964, after testimony was heard on the petition from Willman's attorneys requesting access to additional evidence, Judge Laub ruled the defense was entitled to photographs of the crime scene, witness statements and summaries of police statements taken from Willman.

Judge Laub also ruled on January 28, 1964, that Willman's constitutional rights had not been violated and that the defense's petition to suppress his statements was dismissed.

While the prosecution and Willman's attorneys fought back and forth as the clock ticked down until the hearing, the following day, Erie learned of yet another strangulation murder.

Around three fifteen in the afternoon on January 29, 1964, thirty-five-year-old Edmund Woolslayer, a transport truck driver for Firch's, was en route from Erie to Buffalo, New York, hauling a trailer full of Firch's bread. Woolslayer was passing a snow-covered hemlock grove on Perry Highway when he spotted something on the side of the road.

It looked like a body.

Woolslayer stopped his semi and backed up several feet before getting a closer look. After exiting the semi, he spotted what appeared to be the body of a nude woman, partially obscured behind a fallen tree.

Woolslayer exited his truck and walked into the grove, surrounded by the hemlock trees. The woman was lying on her back with her left arm at her side, her right arm extended above her head. Her legs were bent upward. Nearby, Woolslayer noticed what appeared to be knee prints in the snow near the body.

The sight shook the battle-hardened Korean War veteran to his bones.

"I didn't touch the body," Woolslayer told reporters later that night, still numb. "I knew she was dead."

When asked about the condition of the body, Woolslayer said: "Her face looked as if it had been beaten mercilessly. You've seen someone who has really been hit. Their eyes are black, their nose swollen and everything. That's how she looked."

Woolslayer rushed to the nearby Guild Printing and Lithography building at 5620 Perry Highway and called police.

Detective Tyco Lange arrived first, followed by Detective Leo Weir. Soon, Erie County coroner Wood and additional law enforcement personnel flocked to the scene. Nine feet off the east side of the road, detectives found the torn remnants of what looked like a bra, which they believed belonged to the victim. Nearby, a pair of shoe liners were located. But it was the package of roughly twenty letters, found by police, that seemed like the clue they were looking for. Several of the letters were addressed to a woman named Marian Graham. Other letters bore the return address for the Lyons Transportation Credit Union and loose dollar bills.

Among some of the letters was a postcard sent from Miami Beach, Florida, from someone identified only as "C.J."

A closer inspection of marks in the ground indicated that the body had been dragged to the spot. Nearby, fresh tracks from an automobile were apparent in the snow. The tire tracks, police determined, did not belong to Woolslayer's truck. Detectives then made plaster casts of the tire marks and some of the footprints found near Marian's body.

The woman was identified that night at the morgue as Marian Graham, a forty-two-year-old office manager for the Lyons Transportation Credit Union who usually worked the nine-to-five shift, as well as additional hours on Monday evenings. Marian had been reported missing on the morning of January 28 by her husband, James Lyle Graham.

Marian Graham, born on July 5, 1921, to Fenton and Catherine Yaple, was known well by her neighbors, especially Coroner Wood. A loving wife and mother to her fourteen-year-old son, Marian was known as a "personable, reserved woman" by those who knew her. She also would never stop for or affiliate with strangers.

This indicated that Marian knew her killer.

James Graham told police he last saw his wife the evening before he reported her missing, January 27, around 6:50 p.m., as she was preparing to leave for work. When questioned by police, Graham denied having had any recent quarrels or arguments with his wife. Graham's brother, Wellington Yaple, saw his sister at seven fifteen that evening at a shopping center located at Nineteenth and Peach Streets. Marian told him she would see him at his home that night just after ten o'clock, when she finished her work at the credit union.

A team of detectives, including Detective Sergeant Ray Lapenz from the City of Erie Police Department, were assigned to the case and spread out

Above: Police examine where Marian Graham's body was found. *From left*: Detective Weir, District Attorney Carney and Millcreek police chief Joseph Marshall. *Author's collection.*

Opposite: Marian Graham. *Author's collection.*

in search of Marian. It wasn't long before her car was found abandoned on Summit Street where it intersects with West Twenty-Ninth Street. A search of the trunk revealed a pair of Marian's boots.

Marian's green suede jacket, containing her car keys and purse, was found on Washington Avenue, roughly thirty yards south of the intersection with Lexington Street in nearby Kearsarge. Her purse was found just south of the intersection of Route 19 and Hershey Road.

During the examination of Marian's body and the autopsy that followed, it was noted that her body had several bruises on the thighs and legs, with some swelling on the right cheek. In contrast to the statements made by Edmund Woolslayer, who claimed she looked as if she had been viciously beaten, Wood said the body showed no evidence of "extreme physical violence."

Wood's belief from looking at the body was that Marian's death was a homicide. This was based on the fact that Marian's face was flushed, indicating circulation had been cut off above her neck. Marian's body also showed no signs of being beaten or bound, her skin was not discolored and there were no open wounds. Wood, however, did not entirely discount the possibility that exposure to the cold weather had played a role, indicating further tests were needed before the autopsy was complete.

The preliminary autopsy also found no evidence Marian had been sexually assaulted, but Wood noted that this was difficult to determine due to Marian's body being found in a "semi-frozen state."

It was determined that the Millcreek Police Department would take the lead in the investigation, with detectives from both the state police and City of Erie Police providing assistance.

For police, the murder was too similar to that of Lynn Crotty.

"Is another Daniel Roy Biebighauser on the loose in Erie County?" asked the *Erie Morning News* on January 3, 1964.

Meanwhile, Detective Sergeant Weir searched for L.R. Smith, a male acquaintance of Marian's, who was verified as having been in Erie the Saturday before Graham's death.

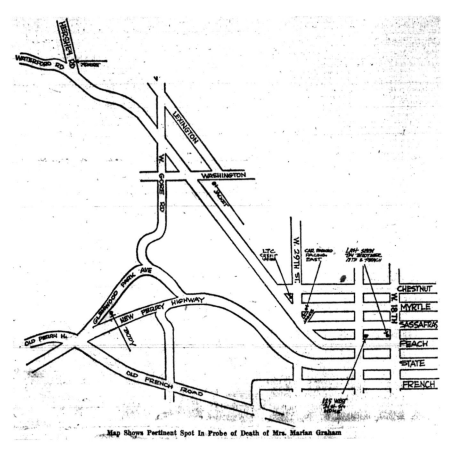

Map Shows Pertinent Spot In Probe of Death of Mrs. Marian Graham

A map showing where items of interest were located in Marian Graham's death. *Erie Daily Times.*

On February 3, Weir acknowledged to reporters that the investigation remained without any strong suspects. The author of the postcards found near Marian's body was also still a mystery—as was the location where she was murdered.

When pressed for answers about where Marian could have been murdered, Weir could only speculate. "Probably in a car somewhere in the city," Weir said with a shrug of his shoulders.

While Detective Sergeant Weir waited for another call from an unidentified woman who had called to report one of the last purported sightings of Marian to police and newspapers, police planned to bring in Joseph Graham again for further questioning. Investigators from the state police and the Millcreek and Erie police planned for a meeting at the detective bureau within the City of Erie Police Department. There, detectives could pool their information and compare notes.

As police reviewed the evidence, they went through Marian's jacket and found a note with a name scribbled on it: Ralph William Rogers.

Detectives also matched Rogers's name to one found on a pad of paper at the credit union where Marian worked; the name had been written there the night she disappeared.

Rogers was no stranger to local law enforcement and had quite a substantial criminal past, all misdemeanors, for the crimes of auto larceny, drunk driving, driving with a suspended license, loitering and prowling.

In each case, Rogers served no jail time.

Brought to the Millcreek police station just after one o'clock in the afternoon, Rogers confessed to being involved in Marian's death after a few minutes of being questioned by detectives, although he claimed he did not kill Marian. Her death, Rogers claimed, was an accident.

Rogers told police that he first met Marian on several occasions in January but denied being intimate with her. It was on Monday, January 27, that Rogers picked up Marian, drove her to an area near where her body was found and parked the car.

Rogers claimed that Marian exited the car and he gave pursuit. At some point, Rogers caught up to Marian and brought her back to his vehicle, when she suddenly screamed and went limp. Pressed further for details, Rogers did not give an explanation as to why she fled from his vehicle in the first place.

After Marian's body went limp, Rogers removed her from the car, carried her across the Perry Highway and threw her body over a guardrail, where it came to rest down a hill in the shallow gully where she was discovered.

When lights from a nearby vehicle thundered down the road, Rogers claimed he became frightened and jumped over the guardrail and into the gully below. After the car vanished, Rogers then dragged Marian's body to the tree where she was later found and disrobed her in an attempt to conceal her from passing motorists.

After this, Rogers continued, he got back into the vehicle and drove south on Perry Highway to the Erie County Thruway, where he reentered Erie via Route 19, scattering Marian's belongings and clothes throughout various locations. Rogers claimed he was back home in Albion by twelve thirty in the morning on January 28. Throughout the entire interrogation, Rogers showed little to no emotion besides a "brief show of tears."

Millcreek police chief Joseph Marshall later noted that Rogers had scratches on his face and wrists when he was arrested by Detective Ray

Investigators photographed behind closed doors while Ralph William Rogers is interrogated. *Author's collection.*

Lapenz and Corporal Williams of the state police. Because of this, scrapings from underneath Marian's fingernails were taken and sent to Harrisburg in an attempt to determine if any trace of skin could be found underneath her nails.

Additional evidence collected at the scene included the casts of the tire marks, which matched those of the vehicle Rogers admitted to driving. Also inside the vehicle was Marian's charge-a-plate, a precursor of what is now known as a credit card.

Later that night, police announced Rogers's arrest during a press conference. District Attorney Carney praised the collaborative work of local law enforcement agencies.

Rogers's statement, however, provided many discrepancies that did not match the evidence. This was confirmed after Rogers was given a polygraph examination and results indicated deception in his answers. It was then that Rogers started to change his statement, now claiming Marian exited his vehicle and ran toward the main highway. Rogers claimed he pursued her and that they both struck the guardrail and fell down the hill.

At the bottom of the hill, Rogers claimed, he fell on top of Marian, who was facedown, and he must have suffocated her while she lay unconscious.

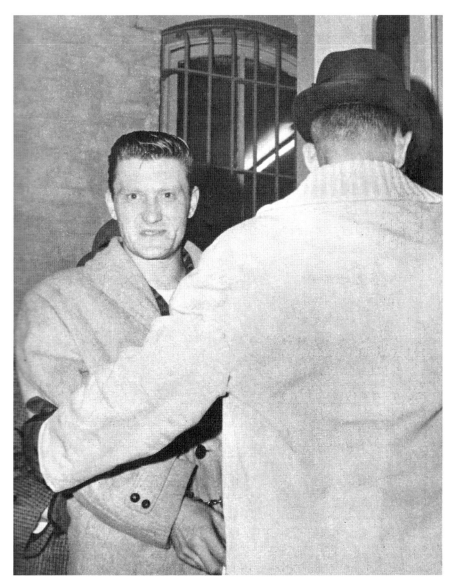

Ralph William Rogers is photographed after his arrest. *Author's collection.*

Rogers was transferred from the Millcreek jail to the county jail late in the night on February 4, 1964. Rogers was without an attorney and had not requested one at this time.

Coroner Wood, indicating his initial reports on Marian's murder were incomplete, still felt that her death was a homicide and hinted he would possibly have to call an inquest, depending on the outcome of additional tests, which were still pending. Chief Deputy Miller of the Erie City Police said to reporters that he had not spoken to Rogers about the Eleanor Free murder.

After Rogers provided his second statement, detectives felt he was not being entirely truthful about how Marian Graham actually died. Police felt there were plenty of details he was not revealing to them.

On the night of February 5, 1964, Coroner Wood announced that Marian Graham died due to asphyxiation caused by manual strangulation, with the ruling made on the advice of St. Vincent Hospital pathologist Richard Eisenberg, who performed the autopsy report. Marian's death occurred, according to Eisenberg, when manual pressure was placed on her larynx, which caused her death.

That night, attorney Lindley R. McClelland was appointed by Judge Burton R. Laub to defend Rogers.

When presented with the details from Marian's autopsy, Rogers continued to profess his innocence. Within several weeks, a divorce was granted to Rogers's estranged wife, Barbara.

As Ralph William Rogers awaited his trial, the February term of criminal court quickly approached, with Willman's trial headlining a total of 109 cases to appear before the court. Days before the trial, Willman's attorneys remained silent regarding how they would proceed with his defense. Expecting the trial to last one and a half to two weeks, the defense counsel subpoenaed forty-five individuals to appear as witnesses, whereas the district attorney subpoenaed twenty-four witnesses to appear.

A brief panic ensued when the district attorney's office was unable to locate witness Charlotte Clugh. Prosecutors issued a subpoena, and the police were tasked with trying to locate her. Clugh later contacted police after learning they were searching for her. She had moved away from Erie and was married under the surname Mossburg.

Those in Erie looked on with morbid curiosity as John Willman's trial began on February 17, 1964.

Chapter 10

JUSTICE DELIVERED

The trial of John Howard Willman began on February 17, 1964, at 9:40 a.m., when the clerk of courts, George L. Wilson, read out loud the murder indictment in courtroom number 1. Willman, dressed in a gray suit, white shirt and darkly shaded red tie, sat with his defense attorneys.

"How do you plead?" Wilson asked.

"The prisoner pleads not guilty," attorney Quinn responded.

The court officers sworn in for the trial included bailiff Harry Vale, Chauncey Isaacson, Wilbur Merritt, Katherine Pancerev and Marian Keinath. Dorothy Petrillo was the court stenographer.

Following Willman's plea, Judge Elmer L. Evans adjourned proceedings to courtroom number 2, where prospective jurors were questioned individually. Defense attorneys asked candidates if they had any problems with returning a verdict of acquittal, as well as questions involving their opinions of police official testimony. District Attorney Carney questioned prospective jurors about their exposure to news of the crime through radio, television or newspapers.

Jury selection continued into the following day, with planned night sessions expected as soon as a full jury was empaneled, which was completed by the afternoon of February 18.

On the morning of February 19, 1964, District Attorney Carney rose from his seat and provided his opening statement to the jury.

"Ladies and gentlemen of the Jury, you have heard many times in this Courtroom over the past several days, this is the case of the Commonwealth

From left: Judge Elmer L. Evans, District Attorney Edward Carney and Assistant District Attorney Richard F. Brabender. *Erie Morning News.*

of Pennsylvania versus John Willman. Mr. Willman is charged with the crime of murder. He's charged with the slaying of Mrs. Laura Mutch on the night of December 30, 1960, in the rear of 717 Holland Street, Erie, Pennsylvania."

Carney outlined the last moments of Laura Mutch's life and how her body was found the following morning. "We will show, ladies and gentlemen, by the medical testimony that she was strangled by her scarf which was placed about her throat and in her mouth and that she was asphyxiated; both the Coroner and the Pathologist will testify to this, and, as a final indignity, this woman sixty-one years of age, this grandmother, was raped."

Carney said the commonwealth planned to show, through witness testimony and Willman's own words in his statements, that the case was proven beyond a reasonable doubt that Willman was responsible for Mutch's murder. "And we will show you by these confessions and by these statements, ladies and gentlemen, that this defendant is guilty of killing Mrs. Mutch. That the killing occurred in the perpetration of the rape of this elderly lady. When we have shown you these facts to your satisfaction we will ask you to find the defendant guilty as charged."

The first witness called to the stand was Detective Captain Carl Kalinowski, who testified about his response to the crime scene and taking photographs of the body, surrounding area and backyard that morning.

Erie County Courthouse. *Erie County Historical Society.*

Charlotte Mossburg described events from the night prior and her subsequent finding of the body the following morning. Following her testimony and cross-examination by Willman's attorneys, court recessed for lunch.

Detective Sergeant Philip Lupo testified how he and his former partner, Detective Carl Malinowski, responded and how the beginning of the investigation unfolded.

Testimony continued into the afternoon, with Coroner Wood discussing his arrival and having the body removed for an autopsy. Dr. John Fust, the pathologist who performed Laura Mutch's postmortem examination and internal and external examinations, discussed how he determined Laura had died from asphyxiation, with additional evidence supporting that she had likely been raped.

Laura Mutch's children, George Meucci and Martha Mutch, were called next and testified what their mother was wearing the night she died and details surrounding the early morning search for her after it was learned she never returned home. The Reverend Richard J. Gibbons, one of the last persons to see Laura alive, discussed how, following the sermon that night, he and his wife spoke to Laura, attempting to give her a ride home, which she declined.

Lucille Kocher, Laura Mutch's granddaughter, testified how she visited 717 Holland Street on the morning of December 31, 1960, with her cousin Lawrence Meucci as a crowd gathered in front of the building. Kocher testified how, while she and her cousin were standing next to each other, they spotted a man whom they identified as John Willman in the area. Kocher also claimed Willman was an acquaintance of the family and knew them.

The next witness was the first of two star witnesses for the prosecution, Davida Boyer.

Boyer recalled, step by step, the frightening assault after Willman offered to take her home and how she managed to escape before police arrived. Irene Fogle provided her testimony, confirming that she witnessed Willman leaving the Tally Ho with Davida Boyer the night she was attacked.

Patrolman William Serafini testified to arriving on the scene and interviewing Davida. Serafini also discussed, in detail, finding Davida's false teeth, glasses and torn underwear. Detective Sergeant Thomas Stanton confirmed that although he obtained a verbal statement from a visibly intoxicated Davida Boyer, he decided to have her incarcerated for the night until a proper statement could be obtained the following day.

THE JURORS WHO WILL DETERMINE WILLMAN'S FATE
No One Knows What Thoughts Might Be Theirs
Sketched at the Trial by Morning News Artist Betsy Nuber

Courtroom sketch by *Morning News* artist Betsy Nuber showing the jurors of Willman's trial. *Erie Morning News*.

Chief witnesses for the prosecution. *From left*: Detective Sergeant McCurdy, Captain DeDionisio, former district attorney Richard Scarpitti and Warden Reeder. *Erie Morning News.*

Following Detective Stanton's questioning, he was excused, and Judge Evans adjourned court for the day at 4:27 p.m. Jurors were transported under supervision to the Richford Hotel.

The fourth day of the trial opened on February 20 with the testimony of Sophia Gorchinsky, who contacted police that morning after Davida was attacked.

After Gorchinsky, District Attorney Carney called Joseph Benacci, Willman's former employer, to the stand. Benacci confirmed for the court that during the previous summer, Willman was employed as a truck driver, a position he had been in for roughly a year. Benacci confirmed to Carney that the green cap found at the scene of the attack belonged to Willman.

Once Joseph Benacci finished his testimony, the second star witness for the prosecution, Detective Sergeant Charles McCurdy, provided his testimony, which took up a large portion of the day. He described how he and his partner, Michael Snider, received a tip from Irene Fogle and arrested Willman before transporting him to the detective bureau. McCurdy explained, in depth, Willman's interrogation and how Willman admitted to the assault of Davida Boyer within a short amount of time.

McCurdy also explained how Willman confessed to killing Laura Mutch and the two statements that were obtained from Willman.

Following a recess for lunch, McCurdy returned to the stand and endured cross-examination by Willman's defense attorneys, who attempted to prove Willman was confused about which crime he was confessing to. Attorney Quinn claimed Willman was not allowed access to an attorney or fed over a long period. McCurdy confirmed, when asked, that Willman never requested to see his family or speak with an attorney.

Despite an objection from Willman's attorneys, Willman's statements were then admitted into evidence by Judge Evans.

Detective Melvin Swanson testified how he and Detective Sergeant McCurdy served a search warrant at the home of Harry and Catherine Willman and discussed Captain DeDionisio's questioning of Willman in the conference room on the night of July 13, 1963.

Mary Warner, an employee of the state department of public welfare, was the next witness and confirmed Willman's address was that of his brother's family in December 1960.

The testimony of Detective Sergeant Michael Snider corroborated McCurdy's in discussing Willman's arrest and the statement obtained that night regarding the assault on Davida Boyer.

Sergeant Curtis Melter of the City of Erie Police provided records showing John Willman was fed while held at the Erie City Jail, which conflicted with the defense's claim that Willman was not fed while held.

Captain Paul J. DeDionisio testified how he assisted in speaking with Willman. DeDionisio denied Willman was mistreated in any way and emphatically stated that over the five days Willman was detained at the police department, he was given every opportunity to deny the crime and told that his statement could be used against him in court.

DeDionisio's testimony hinged on the fact that, despite the numerous warnings, Willman still willingly continued to admit to murdering Laura Mutch.

Former district attorney Richard Scarpitti discussed being informed of Willman's arrest and described how he interviewed Willman and what his initial thoughts on the case were, readily admitting he had reservations about Willman's statement. Scarpitti claimed every precaution was taken to examine the statement and corroborate what Willman confessed to. Willman's second statement, taken in August, was done, Scarpitti claimed, to resolve some concerns that Scarpitti still harbored.

Bruce Reeder, the last witness for the prosecution, confirmed and verified additional documentation. Before resting the prosecution's case, District Attorney Carney entered several items of evidence, which included Willman's hat, Davida Boyer's clothing and the police logs showing when Willman was fed.

At nine fifteen in the morning on February 20, 1963, attorney Bernard F. Quinn presented his opening statement for the defense. In speaking about Willman, Quinn said, "We will prove he did not commit the murder of Mrs. Laura L. Mutch. The murder was committed, but the defendant did not do it."

"John Willman is presumed to be innocent, and we are going to try to show that he could not and did not commit this crime," Quinn concluded.

The first witness called by the defense was Michael DeSantis Jr., the bartender at Huck's Café. DeSantis confirmed he was employed there on December 30, 1960, working from four o'clock in the afternoon to midnight, and also confirmed he was not contacted by police until two weeks prior to the trial. DeSantis confirmed Willman was a frequent customer for the two years prior; however, despite knowing him by sight, he could not recall if Willman was there on December 30. Willman's reputation, DeSantis recalled, was good.

District Attorney Carney took the opportunity to cross-examine DeSantis, attacking DeSantis's inability to remember if Willman was at Huck's Café on December 30, 1960. Despite not seeing Willman there that night, DeSantis did admit to Carney that it was possible Willman was there and he just never crossed paths with him.

Joseph Carl Colangelo, manager of the Hill Mill Dairy in 1960, testified that on the morning Laura Mutch's body was found, he was provided with a frozen footprint and a bottle of a blood-like substance by Detective Kalinowski, who asked for the items to be kept in the dairy's refrigerator. District Attorney Carney objected to Colangelo's testimony, as this information had already been provided through cross-examination during Kalinowski's initial testimony.

Judge Evans overruled Carney's objection and allowed Colangelo to continue.

Attorney Quinn continued to construct the defense's assertion that a prowler, Willman, was operating in the neighborhood that night.

Charlotte Mossberg was recalled to the stand and asked questions about 717 Holland Street and the families who resided there. Attorney Quinn attempted to question her about her upstairs neighbor, Peter Opalensky, but withdrew his question after District Attorney Carney's objection. Mossberg, continuing her testimony, described in detail the backyard of 717 Holland Street and how she located the body.

Sam Campanella, owner of the Tally Ho Bar, recalled seeing both Davida Boyer and John Willman inside the bar the night she was attacked. The bar had been packed that night, Campanella testified, and he confirmed Davida was a reoccurring customer there. Campanella could not confirm if Davida was visibly intoxicated but said if he had seen her intoxicated, he would have shut her off. When she left that night, according to Campanella, she did so under her own power.

Joseph Dominic LaPaglia, a bartender at the Tally Ho, said Davida Boyer visited the bar, on average, about once a week during the day.

LaPaglia testified to hearing Irene Fogle talking about how she identified Davida Boyer's attacker and how she would like to get the reward money. After LaPaglia's testimony concluded, District Attorney Carney asked for it to be stricken and disregarded by the jury due to contradiction on collateral matters, which was agreed to by Judge Evans.

Howard Dobmeier, a photographer, was called to discuss photographs he was asked to take for the defense of the area around 717 Holland Street, including the alleyways and businesses. The photographs were then allowed into evidence. Ann Kopes described how she was awakened during the early morning hours of July 6 by her dog barking. Kopes confirmed that she was unable to see anyone outside her home.

As for a majority of the additional witnesses proposed by Willman's attorneys, Judge Evans ruled against them being called, as they would provide "self-serving declarations." These witnesses, according to Willman's attorneys, would have corroborated testimony from persons inside the Erie County Prison that supported their argument that Willman did not understand why he was incarcerated and was not aware he could request an attorney.

Mrs. Jerry Johnson, an acquaintance of Davida Boyer, testified how Boyer confided in her about the assault and how she believed her attacker also killed Laura Mutch. Before the defense could call its next witness, Judge Evans addressed the jury regarding Johnson's testimony.

"Members of the jury, before we get off this subject, this statement of this lady of the conclusion of Mrs. Boyer concerning who killed who is not important. We admitted it only as it might affect her credibility in what she told you previously, possibly in the hopes of a reward. Whether it affects it or not is up to you, but her conclusion as to Mrs. Mutch, you must disregard because as far as we know now she wasn't there."

Ruth Ann Virginia Rutledge was called next by the defense and told of events that occurred the night of December 30, 1960, while she was working at Scobell's. While she was cleaning inside the building, Rutledge claimed, an unknown older male came to the door asking for a drink. Rutledge told the man to go away and leave her alone. Rutledge testified that a short time later, around nine forty-five, she saw a woman walking in the alleyway with a scarf and a black tweed-like coat on. Then the man who had bothered her returned before disappearing. Rutledge said the man was not John Willman.

Willman's sister-in-law, Carol Willman, testified how she and the family attempted to visit him following his incarceration. As for the night of December 30, 1960, she and her husband went to the home of Harry and Catherine Willman; Carol confirmed her brother-in-law went to bed early that night and did not leave his bedroom while they were present, indicating that if he had attempted to leave, he would have had to pass everyone in order to leave the residence or break through the windows of his room.

Carol also discussed John's upbringing, his service in the national guard and his work for General Electric. The death of his mother, Carol said, had a devastating effect on him.

During cross-examination, District Attorney Carney questioned Carol about John going to bed early that night, asking if there was any possibility he could have left the house without being seen. Carol indicated it would have been difficult for this to happen without anyone present noticing it.

Court then recessed for lunch.

Manuel Rodriguez, the former husband of Catherine Willman, confirmed his children were at the Willman household on December 30, 1960. Catherine Willman testified how she and her husband, Harry, became aware of John's incarceration and confirmed the layout of their home. Catherine claimed John could not even tie his own tie without assistance and testified one of her cousins said some of the men in his company in the national guard had to assist him with his tie and shoes. Carol Willman's mother, Dorothy Beal, testified to John's reputation.

Thomas Kaus provided paperwork from Manpower showing Willman was present the morning of December 31, 1960, and the day prior. Howard E. Smith confirmed he worked with Willman several times at Lake Shore Lumber and acknowledged Willman was present at Manpower at seven o'clock in the morning but that neither Smith nor Willman got any work that day and were released.

Michael J. Selleny, a deputy warden at the Erie County Prison, first met Willman while working at General Electric. Selleny described Willman's reputation as peaceful and discussed what Willman's job duties were at General Electric. John's brothers, Harry and Harold "Eugene" Willman, provided testimony about John's life.

Harry Willman's testimony corroborated that of Catherine and Carol Willman in that John went to bed early that night and never left his bedroom. Harry said the only way John could've left his room was by jumping through the window. These plastic storm windows, Harry continued, were in the rear of the home and were nailed together. If John had attempted to leave through the windows, it would have created considerable noise. Harry confirmed there was no evidence of John attempting to exit through those windows.

Iva Goodwin, a neighbor of Willman's from 1959 through 1960, described his reputation as good.

Kenneth J. Drozeski, a former solder with the Pennsylvania National Guard, told of his time serving with John Willman in the 2nd Battalion of the 112th Infantry Regiment. Drozeski said their fellow soldiers teased Willman and nicknamed him "Baby" because he could not tie his boots and was used as a color-bearer. Drozeski could not recall any instance where Willman posed any disciplinary problems while in the military and testified that, to the best of his knowledge, Willman was shipped overseas with the unit to Germany in September or October 1951.

Dr. Frank J. Pizzat, the psychologist who examined Willman, categorized Willman as a "mild defective" and provided details of his IQ tests, indicating an IQ of sixty-three. Pizzat said Willman was "incapable of reasoning in the abstract, needs to be loved and accepted, and feels quite inadequate, including sexually inadequate." Willman, Pizzat continued, gave off the impression of a person "who is distressed from rejection of others, especially women."

When Pizzat's testimony wrapped up that evening, the defense had called a total of twenty-two witnesses to the stand.

On the morning of Saturday, February 22, 1964, Dr. Michael F. Cleary, a psychiatrist for the Erie Guidance Center, presented his summary of his examination of Willman, which included extensive background on Willman's life. Cleary's report, made on January 7, 1964, included the results of an intelligence test and Cleary's thoughts on Willman's personality, based on his observations after meeting with Willman for a total of five hours between October 1963 and January 1964.

Following Cleary's testimony, Willman's defense attorneys rested their case. Judge Elmer L. Evans provided instructions to the jurors, advising them that they should be allowed as much reading and TV-viewing freedom as possible over the weekend but were not allowed to attend church.

On Sunday, February 23, 1964, jurors were served a chicken dinner at the Erie County Hospital dining room and afterward taken on a "Sunday Drive" to visit various landmarks in the county, including Presque Isle.

Since the selection the prior Monday of the Willman jury, the jurors had remained at the Richford Hotel under guard of court officers and supervised by courthouse law librarian Chauncey Isaken, Katherine Pancerev and

Harry Vale. Careful consideration was also taken to censor stories related to Jack Ruby's trial for murdering Lee Harvey Oswald. Although Judge Evans allowed the jurors to watch television as a group that Saturday night, the televisions in each of the jurors' rooms were disconnected, and they were not allowed access to any newscasts or the courtroom feature *The Defenders*.

In their spare time, the jurors ate together in a separate room, away from the Richford Hotel's main dining area, passing the time playing cards or reading.

On Monday, February 24, 1964, closing arguments began, with District Attorney Edward H. Carney charging that Willman was responsible for Mutch's murder. Attorney Bernard F. Quinn, meanwhile, argued Willman was not responsible for the murder and that the murderer of Laura Mutch was still at large.

"If you convict this man, it will be on the basis of the confessions alone, because that is all the Commonwealth has, and there is serious doubt that Willman was capable of giving the confessions to them," Quinn said to the jury.

Both attorneys completed their summations of the case at eleven o'clock, and Judge Evans began his charge to the jury at twelve forty-five, paraphrasing the case, testimonies, exhibits and evidence presented, as well as the legal points involved. The jury began their deliberations at four o'clock, choosing between four verdicts, ranging from voluntary manslaughter to first-degree murder.

As Willman's family waited for the verdict, they became aware of the issues plaguing him.

"The seriousness of his helplessness was not really known to his family until now," attorney Beveridge later remembered, adding that Willman was incapable of taking care of himself and that should he be acquitted, it would be in his best interest for him to be placed in a state institution for the mentally deficient.

As the hours grew and deliberations progressed, Willman's family were confident of an acquittal.

Harry Willman summed up his feelings to reporters: "We still just think the police got a patsy and that was it. Why, I took John hunting one time and he would not even shoot a deer."

At 6:40 p.m., the jury panel returned to ask Judge Evans for clarification of the differences between first- and second-degree murder and voluntary manslaughter. Judge Evans took seven minutes to present the information, and the jurors retired again, only to return with a verdict an hour and a half later at 8:05 p.m., finding Willman guilty of murder in the first degree.

Following his guilty verdict, John Howard Willman is returned to jail by Deputy Sheriffs Andrew Hanisek and Lou Lazzarine. *Erie Morning News.*

After the verdict, District Attorney Carney asked for mercy for John Willman.

"Society is quite adequately protected with the penalty as it is," Carney said. "I ask that you spare his life."

Following Carney's plea, defense attorneys placed the Reverend James W. Peterson, chaplain of the county prison, on the stand. "He is a very simple man, who has some difficulty in regard to what constitutes right and wrong," Peterson said.

Once Reverend Peterson's testimony was finished, Judge Evans gave his instructions to the jury regarding the penalty to be given. "You have decided the defendant was of sufficient knowledge and purpose in returning the verdict you did. You will use all of what you have heard in setting his penalty."

The jury retired until eight thirty.

Willman sat next to his attorneys, showing little to no emotion or expression, as the jury returned with their decision that Willman would spend the rest of his life in prison.

CHAPTER 11

UNCERTAINTY RESTORED

Following the guilty verdict, attorneys Bernard F. Quinn and James E. Beveridge were left with the question of whether they would file an appeal in response. Beveridge, who was initially hopeful for an acquittal, indicated along with attorney Quinn that any decision for an appeal would need to be made after consulting with Willman's family.

After speaking with Willman's family, Quinn and Beveridge indicated that they would proceed with an appeal, with their arguments focusing on the validity of Willman's detention, his statements and Judge Evans's instructions to the jury. An appeal would be heard before the county court *en banc*—a French term meaning "on the bench," used when all judges of a court hear a case—before Judges Evans, Samuel Y. Rossiter and Burton R. Laub. If the appeal was denied, Willman's attorneys were prepared to fight all the way to the Pennsylvania Supreme Court.

On February 27, 1964, Judge Samuel Y. Rossiter granted a rule to show cause in Willman's appeal. Attorney Quinn was also granted a rule to show cause for his motion in arrest of judgment. In addition to concerns raised about Willman's confession and Judge Evans's points to the jury, Beveridge and Quinn claimed in their petition that the court limited the defendant's psychiatric witnesses in allowing Willman's history, which was not allowed into evidence. The verdict, attorneys Quinn and Beveridge argued, was also contrary to evidence presented. The court scheduled arguments on the rule to show cause to be heard sometime at the end of March.

On April 25, 1963, however, Willman decided to drop his appeal.

"We wanted to go forward with the appeal," said Harry Willman. "But John didn't want to take a chance on getting the chair."

After his conviction, once Willman was told an appeal would present a risk of him being retried, with a possible death sentence, Willman, who claimed he was tormented in the county prison by other inmates saying he would get the chair, decided to not proceed.

Attorney Quinn told reporters, "This is probably the first time in his life he's ever been able to take a position and insist on holding it."

With the threat of the electric chair no longer hanging over his head, the thought of life imprisonment brought comfort to John Howard Willman as he sat alongside his attorney, his siblings and District Attorney Edward H. Carney in Judge Evans's chambers. Once Willman reiterated his request to drop his appeal, Judge Evans committed Willman to the Western Correctional Diagnostic and Classification Center in Pittsburgh, Pennsylvania.

Regardless of the fact that Willman had withdrawn his appeal, two additional motions filed by his attorneys—a motion for a new trial and a motion to arrest the jury's verdict—were still pending before the court.

John Howard Willman speaks with his family. *From left*: Carol Willman, Catherine Willman and Harry Willman. Eugene Willman has his back to the camera. *Erie Daily Times*.

John Howard
Willman is
escorted from Erie
County Prison by
Deputy Sheriff
Andrew Hanisek.
Erie Daily Times.

In the days before his removal to Western Penitentiary, Willman visited with his siblings, savoring what he could of his last days of freedom.

Around eight o'clock in the morning on April 30, 1964, Willman was escorted from the Erie County Prison. Photographers were there as Willman exited, handcuffed, with a cigarette hanging from his mouth as he was placed into a waiting vehicle. Willman would be accompanied to Pittsburgh by deputy Erie County sheriffs William Parker and Andrew J. Hanisek. Also joining them was *Erie Morning News* reporter Bill Campbell.

The trip south was uneventful, and Willman's silence gradually dissipated into small talk and jokes. It was when the group reached the front entrance to Western Penitentiary that Willman's jovial attitude disappeared. Willman was said to have been visibly shaken by the towering stone walls and large metal doors as the men entered the prison.

Inside one of the reception rooms of the penitentiary, Willman looked around nervously while Deputy Hanisek finished the required paperwork to finalize the transfer.

Willman commented to Bill Campbell about his treatment in Erie. "Those turnkeys treated me nice. I'm going to miss them." Willman told Campbell he hoped someday he would be able to go to a prison farm where he could work outside.

Asked for final remarks, Willman replied: "Someday, I hope, the real story will come out. I swear I didn't do it."

Willman said his final goodbyes to Deputy Hanisek, his voice breaking with emotion. "You'll do all right here, Johnny," Hanisek responded, shaking Willman's hand and patting him on the back.

And with that, flanked by prison guards, John Howard Willman shuffled along the main corridor until he vanished from view. Bill Campbell, gathering his notes for the *Morning News*, questioned Warden James Maroney. In regard to Willman's statements maintaining his innocence, Maroney replied, "Of the 1,000 inmates we have here now, 180 are serving life terms for murder. A vast majority of them say they never killed anyone."

On July 22, 1964, the *Erie Daily Times* reported that Erie County judges had approved final expenses for the Willman trial, totaling $2,692, fixing total counsel fees for the court-appointed defense attorneys at $1,350, with $675 reimbursed for each attorney. The court also approved additional expenses for $1,342 in response to defense expenses securing additional investigation, photos and professional testimony in the case, with money being paid directly to the persons whose services were utilized.

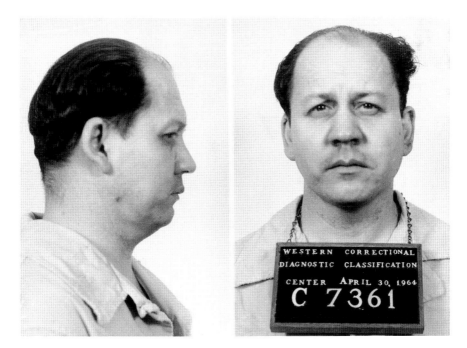

John Howard Willman poses for his mug shot at Western State Penitentiary. *Pennsylvania State Archives.*

In their petition for allowance of expenses and fees, Quinn and Beveridge told the court they each spent 260 hours in preparation for the case. The court did refuse to pay five dollars in witness fees for each of the fifteen persons called to testify for the defense in the case.

Willman appears to have had a change of heart by November 1964, when he requested copies of his court transcripts, a move that was believed to be his first step in preparing for an appeal.

On November 15, 1964, Willman's attorneys told the *Times* they had not been contacted about any plans for an appeal, with Beveridge feeling Willman's chances for an appeal had improved following a recent decision by the Pennsylvania Supreme Court. The decision, written by Justice Samuel J. Roberts, a former Orphans Court judge from Erie, was in regard to *Commonwealth ex rel. O'Lock, Appellant, v. Rundle* (1964).

Justice Roberts wrote, "Only counsel may adequately protect the interests of the criminal defendant. Such counsel, if desired, must be afforded. The constitution demands no less." This decision, once issued, granted writs of habeas corpus to eleven convicts who, after appearing in court without counsel, claimed they had been deprived of their constitutional rights. The controlling case involved a petition by convict John O'Lock of Dauphin County, who had been serving time for burglaries and additional offenses since pleading guilty in 1944.

The Pennsylvania Supreme Court's decision opened the floodgates for hundreds of prisoners claiming they had been held without counsel and, in accordance with the decision, were deprived of their constitutional rights. Erie County assistant district attorney William A. Pfeiffer told the *Times* they had received so many petitions, it would be a full-time job for one of the assistants within the district attorney's office to handle them. Numerous attorneys in Erie indicated a public defender system would be the only adequate way of addressing the petitions in response.

The Willman case would continue to attract the local press as 1964 came to a close, with *Times* reporter Garth Minegar writing an editorial about recent criticism of the free press and the argument against it being an enemy of fair trials.

Using the recent denial of a murder conviction in New Jersey, where the appeal was denied on grounds of "trial by newspaper," Minegar wrote about Willman's attorneys attempting to quash his indictment based on the grounds that the jurors would have been influenced by reports of his indictment fourteen hours before it became a confirmed fact.

Erie's newly constructed city hall as it would have appeared in 1964. *Erie County Historical Society.*

Minegar confirmed that the actions of the grand jury were known by local reporters six hours prior to being broadcast but maintained the *Times* refused to publish them on the basis that the indictment was not presented before the judge in the proper judicial process.

With Willman behind bars in the Western Penitentiary, the rest of the world moved on. On April 29, 1965, fifty-four-year-old Davida Boyer, who survived an attack by John Willman, died at Hamot Hospital, succumbing to pulmonary metastasis. She was buried in Erie Cemetery.

In June 1966, John Howard Willman wrote a petition asking for release from custody, correction of sentencing and a new trial. In his handwritten petition, Willman wrote that he was not represented by counsel when arrested and, interestingly, claimed he was not represented by counsel until a few days prior to his trial. Willman wrote that the state used evidence obtained illegally—the evidence being his statements—which Willman argued were obtained through coercion, and that his constitutional rights were violated.

Erie County district attorney Lindley McClelland was tasked with responding to Willman's petition and was ordered by Erie County judges Elmer L. Evans and James B. Dwyer to submit an answer within twenty days.

Willman's appeal requesting a new trial came at a time when Erie County was dealing with a new state law, which went into effect on March 1, 1966. The law redefined procedures for post-conviction hearings of defendants who appealed their cases. This new rule was met with disdain from local officials, who claimed such rules would cause additional expenditures, which the county was not prepared to handle with that year's budget.

The new laws also created tremendous strain on the public defender's office. Attorney Dana Sherwood Jones told the *Times* that if counsel was ordered by the court for a defendant for a hearing, he would handle the extra workload unless directed otherwise, and he confirmed that there would be no additional incurred budget costs for the public defender's office.

This law forced the district attorney's office to hire a sixth assistant, creating the largest staff for the district attorney's office in history at the time. Although the paperwork would not be as extensive as once believed, it presented time limits on second and third appeals directed at the higher courts.

Dana Sherwood Jones was appointed to represent John Howard Willman on July 15, 1966, for his appeal.

Known as "Sher" by fellow attorneys, Dana Sherwood Jones was born and raised in Erie, Pennsylvania. A noted Eagle Scout and graduate of Academy High School in 1938, Jones attended Ohio State University before serving in World War II in the Eleventh Infantry Regiment, where he achieved the rank of captain while serving in all five European campaigns.

When serving in Ireland during the war, Jones met his future wife, Margaret Rodgers. Following the war, Jones returned to Ireland, where he married Margaret, and he later returned stateside with her. Following his return, Jones attended the University of Michigan Law School, graduating in 1949 before finding his way back to Erie, where he became the city's first public defender in 1965. A fervent believer that everyone, regardless of their creed, deserved a fair and proper trial in accordance with the United States Constitution, Jones's ethic earned him respect and praise.

With the appeal process started, Irene Fogle, now married, presented a claim through her attorney, Gerald A. McNelis Sr., to claim the $500 reward in the Mutch case. In a letter presented to the Erie County commissioners, McNelis stated Fogle's identification of Willman led to his arrest and warranted her legal right to recoup the reward as offered. Erie County's commissioners responded they would await a recommendation from the district attorney before proceeding.

As anticipated, on December 1, 1966, District Attorney McClelland asked the county commissioners to withhold the reward until the case was officially closed, claiming Willman's appeal deemed the case still open.

Dana Sherwood Jones spent several months reviewing Willman's petition from 1966 for a new trial and met with him several times, poring through copies of the 1964 trial records. On April 27, 1963, attorney Jones filed a petition seeking Willman's release from custody, along with correction of his sentence and a new trial. Responding to the petition, Assistant District Attorney Michael A. Palmisano argued Willman's confession was legally obtained without violating his rights. Palmisano, responding on behalf of the Erie County district attorney's office, also argued Willman was not detained illegally nor denied his right to counsel.

As Jones prepared the next steps in Willman's appeal, attorney Vedder White was brought on to assist. A native of Albany, New York, White later moved with his family to Erie, where he graduated from Cathedral Prep. After graduating from Villanova University and the Charles Widger School of Law, White returned to Erie, where he worked for the public defender's office.

District Attorney Richard Brabender, who became district attorney after his predecessor, Lindley R. McClelland, was appointed as a judge in 1967, was tasked with responding to the petition by May 5. Because of the complexity of the case, Brabender was granted a ten-day extension for his response.

On June 15, 1967, Judge Lindley R. McClelland heard arguments on whether he should disqualify himself from hearing the appeal. Attorney Jones asked for the recusal based on McClelland's response to Willman's posttrial application for relief in 1966, when he was serving as district attorney.

Judge McClelland presided before defense attorneys Jones and White, along with District Attorney Brabender and Assistant District Attorney Palmisano, on June 30, 1967. Attorneys Jones and White provided their arguments, heavily relying on *Davis v. State of North Carolina* (1966), with attorney White claiming Willman's written admissions should be considered illegal since no right of counsel was presented to Willman and the statements were extracted without benefit of counsel.

Davis v. North Carolina (1966) dealt with a defendant who was arrested after escaping a North Carolina state prison. The defendant, taken into custody in connection with a murder investigation, was kept in a detention cell for sixteen days. During this time, the defendant only spoke to the police. The defendant confessed to the crime, and there was no record of him being advised of his rights until after his confessions. During the trial, the written confession and testimony regarding an oral confession were introduced into evidence despite objections from defense attorneys that the confessions were obtained involuntarily.

The defendant was found guilty and sentenced to death. The United States Supreme Court later ruled the confessions were obtained involuntarily due to coercive influences and were considered constitutionally inadmissible as evidence. The Supreme Court later wrote that the "uncontested fact that no one other than the police spoke to the defendant during his 16 days' detention and interrogation is significant in determining voluntariness."

Attorney White presented evidence that suggested police used psychological coercion to their advantage with Willman's extended imprisonment. Willman's mental deficiency and low IQ of 63 also played a role in him readily confessing to the murder, White argued. Asked whether the defense was disputing Willman's admission following his arrest, White responded that the defense's argument was in reference to the two written confessions.

District Attorney Brabender argued Willman's confessions were not illegal in accordance to the right to counsel, which followed the groundbreaking cases of *Miranda v. Arizona* (1966) and *Escobedo v. Illinois* (1964), cases that defined guidelines on this point. These cases, Brabender argued, were decided after Willman's case and were not retroactive. When questioned about the argument that Willman involuntarily provided his confessions, Brabender pointed out that Willman had been kept in jail while police determined if he was telling the truth about the murder of Laura Mutch.

Brabender echoed the words of Captain DeDionisio when he said every opportunity was presented for Willman to be truthful and not to confess to the murder if he did not commit it. Dismissing the defense's arguments as "allegations," both Palmisano and Brabender argued the defense relied too heavily on *Davis v. North Carolina* and that both cases were entirely different.

Judge McClelland asked "whether, if he decided the statements really involuntary, he should grant a new trial even though the defense was not questioning the validity of the oral admission."

Brabender admitted there should be a new trial if Willman's written confessions were ruled invalid. Following the arguments, Judge McClelland postponed further consideration of the motion for a new trial to allow Brabender's office time to respond to the defense's arguments.

Judge McClelland dismissed Willman's petition for immediate release from confinement on July 27, 1967, telling attorneys Jones and White to instead file a motion for a new trial for consideration by the court en banc. McClelland, responding to Willman's argument that his release should be granted under the Post-Conviction Hearing Act of January 26, 1966, said Willman had to show "error resulting in his conviction and sentence has not been finally litigated or waived."

"Finally litigated," McClelland continued, "means it has been raised in trial court, the trial court has ruled on the merits of the issue, and the petitioner has knowingly understandingly failed to appeal the trial court's ruling."

McClelland pointed to the fact that when Willman waived his right to a new trial, any alleged errors argued were considered finally litigated, and there would be no further remedy available under the Post-Conviction Hearing Act because of his constitutional issues raised at the 1963 hearing before Judge Burton R. Laub and during the trial in 1964. "The trial court ruled adversely on the merits of the issues," McClelland stated. "And Willman failed to appeal."

Judge McClelland did state "several fascinating constitutional problems are alleged. The court is reluctant to close the door of an appeal to John Willman," and advised Willman that if he was not satisfied, he could appeal to the Pennsylvania Supreme Court.

On July 28, 1967, attorney Dana Sherwood Jones petitioned the court for a new trial on three points of law, filing the petition before Judge McClelland. "We have to go over the entire record again, this time with a fine-tooth comb," Jones told reporters.

The following day, Judge McClelland granted a rule to show cause for a motion for retrial, setting the stage for the case to be presented before the county court en banc, which would include Judges McClelland, Thomas W. Barber and Elmer L. Evans, with Judge Edward H. Carney excusing himself. On December 21, 1967, it was announced that the hearing would be held on January 23, 1968.

On January 23, 1968, attorneys Jones and White presented their case before Judges McClelland, Evans and Barber, arguing Willman had a lack of counsel for seventy-five days and that his statements were involuntary and were grounds for a new trial. Several pretrial circumstances supported their argument that the statements were involuntary; these included Willman's prolonged detention, his intensive interrogation, law enforcement's failure to advise Willman of his rights, his lack of a proper diet, the absence of proper resting quarters and the failure to allow friends and relatives to see the defendant while incarcerated.

Willman's confession, obtained on August 30, 1963, fifty days after Willman's arrest, represented a gross neglect of Willman's constitutional rights, according to Jones and White. This all hinged on the fact that the case against Willman relied solely on his confessions. It was argued that without these confessions, which the defense believed were illegally obtained, there was no physical evidence connecting Willman to the murder of Laura Mutch.

Issuing a fifteen-page opinion on May 2, 1968, Erie County judges McClelland, Evans and Barber granted John Willman a new trial based on the grounds that his confession was invalid and obtained involuntarily.

The judges wrote:

> *Tested by 1968 standards of voluntariness, the written confession of John H. Willman, taken in the Erie County Jail on August 31, 1963 (49 days after his arrest) without benefit of counsel, without adequate warnings of his constitutional rights, with full knowledge that (he) was a mental defective, is an invalid and involuntary confession.*

It was the first time in Erie County Court history that a murder defendant had been granted a new trial.

Following the granting of a new trial, Judge Thomas W. Barber appointed attorney Will J. Schaaf to aid Willman's defense. As Willman's attorneys prepared for his upcoming retrial, John Willman, now forty-one and incarcerated at the Pennsylvania State Penitentiary in Huntington, was returned to Erie County on July 9 regarding his attorney's petition to suppress the statements he made following his arrest in 1964.

Attorneys Schaaf and White argued before Judge McClelland that higher court rulings regarding confessions had been applied for retrials, citing the cases of *Escobedo* and *Miranda*. Judge McClelland ruled in August, however, that he would defer the motion to suppress Willman's confessions until trial, saying that due to the ever-changing nature of such cases, "this court will decide the matter on the basis of the cases now in existence."

With the fall of 1968 approaching, John Willman's retrial revived the public's attention to and morbid curiosity about the crowded session of the Erie County Criminal Court starting on September 9, 1968.

In the halls of the Erie County Courthouse, however, the upcoming trial was called something else.

The Second Battle of Lake Erie.

Chapter 12

THE SECOND BATTLE
OF LAKE ERIE

A pretrial conference was held on September 15, 1968, before Judge Lindley R. McClelland, with both the defense and prosecution present. District Attorney William "Bill" Pfadt, who won the election for the role in 1967, appointed former district attorney Richard F. Brabender as special prosecutor. Together, he and Assistant District Attorney Michael Palmisano would lead the prosecution. Leading Willman's defense would be attorneys Will J. Schaaf and Vedder White.

The conference carried over until the following day and focused on "very complicated and very touchy points of the law," an unnamed legal expert said to the *Erie Daily Times*, with prosecutors claiming that even if Willman's confessions were ruled as inadmissible, they would proceed with the trial.

Another difficulty for the prosecution was the fact that Davida Boyer was now deceased, although it was expected her testimony from 1964 would be sworn into the record, a move that was expected to be challenged by Willman's attorneys.

In a blow to the defense, Judge McClelland denied their request to suppress Willman's confessions.

Jury selection began at ten o'clock in the morning on Wednesday, September 17, 1968, with questioning of prospective jurors expected to last throughout the day in courtroom number 3. With the questioning lasting around sixteen minutes per person, defense attorneys asked if participating in a retrial would affect prospective jurors' opinions. The prospective jurors were also asked their opinions of police testimony compared to that of ordinary citizens. Prosecutors focused their questions on the influence of the media along with the personal opinions of the jurors.

Out of thirty-three persons questioned that day, only two were seated on the jury panel, and jury selection continued into Thursday, September 19. The trial, in its fourth day, had seen the questioning of sixty-eight individuals. As attorneys were running out of jurors, Judge McClelland ordered deputies from the Erie County Sheriff's Department to gather twenty random citizens for jury duty. Additionally, twelve individuals selected were pooled from a previous trial that had ended the day before. By the end of the day, a jury of eight women and four men, along with two alternative jurors, was sworn in.

On September 20, 1968, after an opening statement presented by Richard Brabender, Carl Kalinowski was called to the stand and testified with in-depth knowledge of the crime scene at 717 Holland Street. Kalinowski also positively identified the Bible, eyeglasses and buttons found in the backyard of 717 Holland Street, confirming that they were the same seen at the crime scene on the morning of December 31, 1960.

Brabender was attempting to have exhibits A through F admitted into testimony when attorney Schaaf objected. "Your Honor, we have no objections to the exhibits up through E and F. We are compelled by our Supreme Court decision in the Commonwealth versus Eckert to object to E and F."

In the case of *Commonwealth v. Eckert*, a conviction had been overturned due to photographs that were ruled inflammatory.

Judge McClelland admitted exhibits A, B, C and D into evidence while attorney Schaaf and District Attorney Brabender approached in a sidebar. Exhibits E and F, contested by the defense, were photographs of Laura Mutch's body with the handkerchief still wrapped around her face.

"These photos were blown up out of proportion, and by their very magnitude are unduly inflammatory, prejudicial, and unnecessary to the prosecution of this case," Schaaf said in a hushed voice.

"Exhibit F is being introduced for the purpose of being shown the manner in which the scarf or kerchief of Mrs. Mutch was pulled through her mouth, around the back of her neck and tied, and it becomes very, very important for the testimony that will follow," Brabender retorted.

Because the photographs showed the back of Laura Mutch's head and neck, not her face, Judge McClelland admitted the photographs into evidence, and after verification, the photographs were shown to the jury. Kalinowski continued his testimony, identifying the scarf wrapped around Mutch's mouth and throat and confirming for the commonwealth that all evidence was kept in a police department safe until 1964 and, following the first trial, was kept by the district attorney's office.

Attorney Schaff cross-examined Kalinowski, asking if he made attempts to obtain fingerprints.

"There was nothing you could take fingerprints of at the scene," Kalinowski responded.

"Let me ask this," Schaaf continued. "What about the body of the deceased, were you able to get any prints from the body?"

"No."

"Did you try?"

"We tried on the glasses, there was nothing on the glasses."

Kalinowski acknowledged that police attempted to use an iodine fumer to locate fingerprints on the first page of the Bible, but these attempts were unsuccessful. Kalinowski took the time to explain to the jury how the process worked and what they were looking for, admitting that due to the texture of the Bible's cover, it was difficult to locate a fingerprint and match one.

The only piece of evidence Kalinowski felt could have been listed as a print was visible in one of the photographic exhibits, which showed a possible knee print caused by someone sliding on the ice, the mark having been frozen over.

Called next was Laura Mutch's son, George Meucci. Meucci testified to the events of December 30 when he dropped his mother off at the Gospel Tabernacle Church. Meucci testified how he received a call from his sister around three o'clock in the morning, reporting their mother never returned home, and concluded his testimony by telling of his visit to 717 Holland Street and the identification of his mother's body.

Laura Mutch's daughter, Martha Mutch, was called and identified her mother's clothing and Bible. This series of testimonies, which mirrored those given in 1964, continued with the testimony of the Reverend Richard Gibbons.

After a short recess at 11:00 a.m., Charlotte Mossburg testified finding Laura Mutch's body behind her duplex that morning. After Mossburg finished her testimony for the commonwealth, attorney Schaff cross-examined her, asking her about the difficulties at the time dealing with prowlers in the neighborhood.

Brabender objected to the question about prowlers in the neighborhood. "I ask for an offer of proof concerning this cross examination, it's beyond the scope of the direct examination."

"All right," Judge McClelland said, easing back into his chair. "Do you wish to make an offer of proof?"

"No, I thought it was a fair question," Attorney Schaaf countered.

"I don't think it's a fair question at this moment," Judge McClelland responded. "If you wish to make an offer of proof and can show me why it is, I will hear it. It's far beyond the scope of the direct examination."

The objection being sustained by Judge McClelland, attorney Schaaf promptly ended his cross-examination. Judge McClelland took the opportunity to explain to the jury the reason for the objection being sustained. Right out the gate, Willman's attorneys were finding it difficult to prove the possibility that other criminals were operating in the neighborhood on the night of December 30, 1960.

Called next to the stand was Lieutenant Phillip Lupo.

Lupo described how he and Carl Malinowski originally were called to 717 Holland Street. After confirming the items submitted into evidence, Lupo described the intricate way the scarf was tied around Laura Mutch's mouth. Attorney Schaaf took the opportunity during cross-examination to point out footprints in the area that could have been made the night prior. Lupo was unable to confirm how or when any of these footprints in the backyard of 717 Holland Street had been made.

At that point, although the testimonies continued to be similar to those in 1964, Willman's defense attorneys decided to not only attack the confessions but also try to figure out different ways that they could prove there was reasonable doubt that Willman was responsible.

After Lupo stepped down from the stand, Ruth Amerlind of the Erie County Board of Assistance was called to provide testimony confirming Willman's place of residence, listed as 452 East Eighth Street, a fact not contested by Willman's attorneys.

Following a recess for lunch, defense attorneys and prosecutors met in Judge McClelland's chambers, due to attorney Schaaf announcing that the defense planned on objecting to the grandchildren of Laura Mutch being called as witnesses and telling of how they identified Willman outside 717 Holland the morning Laura Mutch's body was discovered. Judge McClelland was also presented with the dilemma about Davida Boyer's testimony, with Judge McClelland advising attorneys he would read the testimony and determine what was objectionable.

Further arguments ensued between attorneys Brabender and Schaaf when Brabender inquired about how far he could explain why Willman was arrested and brought to the department. Schaaf objected, saying he believed such a statement would be highly prejudicial to the jury since Willman had not been convicted of the attack on Davida Boyer.

Attorney Schaaf argued that between the murder of Laura Mutch and getting into details involving the attack on Davida Boyer almost three years later, the jury would have a difficult time separating the two.

"I have to have some basis for reaching this testimony," Brabender said.

"You will be allowed to tell the court that she is now deceased and she testified under oath on cross examination at the trial," McClelland ordered. Judge McClelland told all attorneys he would rule on additional matters as they were presented to the court.

Eighteen-year-old Lucille Kocher and twenty-one-year-old Lawrence Meucci were called to the stand and told the court how they had walked down to the home of their grandmother. It was around East Seventh or Eighth Street that both of them saw police and spectators crowded outside 717 Holland Street. Near the corner of the block, both testified to seeing a man who asked what had happened. Kocher identified John Willman and recognized him as an acquaintance of the family prior to her grandmother's murder.

Erie County coroner Merle Wood and pathologist Dr. John Fust were then called and testified about how Laura Mutch was found and the details surrounding her body's removal from the scene and the autopsy that followed. The next witness called to the stand was Charles A. McCurdy, now a lieutenant, and Detective Michael J. Snider.

Both men testified to Willman's oral confession after he was arrested and the two additional confessions that followed. McCurdy read, into the record, Willman's two-page statement, signed by Willman.

The following day, September 21, 1968, Paul J. DeDionisio, now a chief county detective, testified that Willman was told he had constitutional rights and was warned he did not have to speak to the police before making a written confession.

Willman, DeDionisio told the court, admitted the crime after numerous warnings were given. Willman's attorneys attempted to attack DeDionisio's testimony through cross-examination; however, DeDionisio withstood the attempts to take apart his testimony, defending his attempts to warn Willman and advise him of his rights and asserting that they were made with sincerity. DeDionisio's testimony, along with that of McCurdy, was viewed as the most crucial for the prosecution.

Willman's attorneys were aware of this, knowing that the voluntariness of the statements, coupled with how Willman was indefinitely held, in conjunction with his mental disabilities, all played a role in Willman confessing to the murder—or at least that was the angle they continued to try to present to the court and jury.

Although Willman's attorneys attempted to shatter the testimonies of police officials, they fell short of making a dent in the prosecution's case, which did not go unnoticed by those present in the courtroom.

Former district attorney Richard Scarpitti was called to provide testimony to explain why he delayed charging Willman with the murder. Scarpitti's reservations, he testified, were because of a desire to have it medically established that the confession was not simply the result of neurosis or psychosis and that it was truthful and supported by details only the killer would have known.

After the prosecution rested, attorney White presented his opening statement, indicating Willman had an IQ of 63, which meant none of his alleged confessions could be taken seriously. White stressed Willman could be "molded like putty." Following testimony that lasted into the evening hours, court was adjourned at eleven thirty, with plans to convene the following Monday, September 23, 1968.

That Monday, Detective Melvin Swanson provided testimony about Willman's questioning on July 14, 1963. "John was a hard man to interrogate; he wouldn't initiate a conversation," Swanson said.

Swanson testified how Willman confessed to the murder of Laura Mutch after admitting to the attack on Davida Boyer. Deputy Chief Miller also testified about events that transpired, with attorney Schaaf questioning both men under cross-examination. Deputy Chief Miller confirmed he knew of three inaccuracies in the statement that Willman provided.

Schaaf asked Miller why these inaccuracies were allowed.

"This is Mr. Willman's statement. He said this." Miller pointed to the statements, noting that detectives typed verbatim what Willman was responding to with his answers.

Following closing arguments presented by both the prosecution and the defense, Judge McClelland presented his instructions to the jury. "I think in this case you could conclude that Laura Mutch was raped. The only question is whether Mr. Willman did it or not."

Three and a half hours after the jury received instructions from the judge and began deliberations, attorneys were notified the jury had already reached a "compromise" verdict. At eight fifteen, the verdict was read, with John Howard Willman again being found guilty, this time of second-degree murder.

Following the guilty verdict, attorneys Schaaf and White contended the court erred when it did not suppress Willman's oral and written statements from his interrogation in July 1963, arguing the standard of the U.S. Supreme Court's *Miranda* and *Escobedo* cases did in fact apply to retrials.

Shortly after nine o'clock in the morning on September 26, 1968, catching courthouse aides and observers off guard, John Howard Willman was sentenced by Judge McClelland to serve ten to twenty years in the Western Penitentiary and fined an additional $500. The sentencing had come exactly five years to the day after he was originally charged in the case in 1963.

Willman's attorneys indicated that they would file an immediate appeal to the Pennsylvania Supreme Court.

On October 4, 1968, in an eleven-page opinion by Erie County judge Lindley R. McClelland, in agreement with Judge James B. Dwyer, the retrial motion for John Howard Willman was denied in a move that "bucked the State Supreme Court and called upon the U.S. Supreme Court for 'final word' on applicability of limitations of confessions in retrials." according to the *Erie Daily Times*.

Judge McClelland wrote:

> *Practically speaking, it seems absurd to hold that the police should have given warnings in 1963 which were unheard of until 1964 and 1966. Practically speaking, it seems ridiculous to apply Miranda to retrials.*
>
> *The law, however, moves in strange ways it's wonders to perform. Many courts have applied Miranda to retrials.*
>
> *It is the view of this court that the final word should come from the Supreme Court of the United States. Until that court speaks, it is our hope that the Supreme Court of Pennsylvania will consider the problem anew and in the final analysis conclude that Miranda does not apply to retrials.*

The denial of a retrial drew condemnation from attorneys Schaaf and White, who announced the decision would be immediately appealed to the state supreme court.

On December 13, 1969, Armand Chimenti, now chief of the City of Erie Police Department, met with Martin Siegel, a representative of *Official Detective Stories* magazine, as the Meritorious Service Citation award was presented to the City of Erie Police Department for the Laura Mutch investigation. That month, an article written by Harold Whitby, titled "The Pennsylvania Killer-Rapist Wore Ladies Undies," appeared in the January 1969 issue.

The Pennsylvania Supreme Court heard arguments on January 8, 1969, from Willman's defense attorneys, who maintained Willman's confessions should not have been admitted into evidence in the second trial. Any chance that Willman or his defense attorneys had of being able to get the Pennsylvania

Martin Siegel (*left*), representative of *Official Detective Stories*, presents Chief Chimenti with the Meritorious Service Citation award to City of Erie Police. *Erie Daily Times*.

Supreme Court or the United States Supreme Court to overturn the second conviction was extinguished when, in June 1969, the United States Supreme Court ruled that the precedent-setting *Miranda* decision did not apply to retrials for older cases.

Judge McClelland praised the confirmation:

> *This is in my opinion one of the most important opinions of the Warren Court. The lower courts have been left hanging since the Miranda rule in 1966, and there have been a number of varying opinions as to how it would apply to retrials of cases that occurred prior to the date of the ruling.*

The *Times* joined Judge McClelland in supporting the confirmation that *Miranda* would not apply to older, previous cases.

Noting that Judge McClelland had risked his judicial reputation in denying Willman a new trial in regard to how *Miranda* would be enforced—especially as he was dealing with a case that had occurred prior to the Supreme Court's ruling, which could have been overturned—the *Times* added Willman was, regardless, still found guilty by a jury of his peers, "with the knowledge that he is a mental defective."

Several weeks later, on July 2, 1969, the Pennsylvania Supreme Court upheld the denial of a new trial and, in a decision written by Justice Samuel Roberts, agreed *Miranda* was not retroactive to older cases. The high court justices did disagree on the voluntariness of Willman's confession, with Justice Henry J. O'Brien of Pittsburgh writing in his dissenting opinion that the questioning of Willman for five hours at a time and holding him for four days led him to believe that Willman's confession was obtained involuntarily. Despite this, Judge O'Brien agreed the *Miranda* decision was not retroactive.

Despite the Pennsylvania Supreme Court's denial to grant John Willman a new trial, attorneys White and Schaaf petitioned the federal court in Erie for a writ of habeas corpus "on grounds that confessions introduced into evidence against him at the time of his trial were involuntarily taken and in violation of his constitutional rights."

Both attorneys were directed to file a brief on all questions of law affecting their petition by October 1, with an answer from the district attorney's office to be filed no later than October 10. Federal judge Gerald J. Weber would then decide on whether an evidentiary hearing was necessary or whether court records and briefs were sufficient for a ruling on the defense's petition.

The additional moves by Willman's attorneys, however, proved fruitless as the petition for a writ of habeas corpus was denied.

Since the fall of 1960, Erie and its citizens had been plagued by endless reports of attacks against women in a saga that stretched out for almost a decade. The case against John Howard Willman was the last in the series of attacks against women in which the person responsible was convicted.

Following the last moves by Willman's attorneys in the fall of 1969, the cases of attacks against women in Erie vanished from the papers as everyone focused on a new decade.

The 1970s.

The fear and terror finally ended.

CHAPTER 13

EPILOGUE

I n the fifty-three years since John Howard Willman's second conviction in 1969, Erie has changed drastically. The 1960s began as a promising decade for the city, as it saw its largest-yet population of 138,440. Erie also was a finalist for the All-American City Award in 1961 but lost to Lynwood, California.

Despite being an industrious manufacturing town, Erie, like many other cities, would suffer the effects of the restructuring of manufacturing with dwindling steel and coal production. By 1970, the city had suffered a 6.7 percent decline in its population. The opening of the Millcreek Mall Complex in 1975, along with downtown retail businesses closing, caused many to leave the city, heading to the neighboring suburbs.

These changes, similar to those in other Rust Belt cities, have continued on a downward trend ever since.

Erie's commercial fishing industry was also hit hard and today is almost nonexistent; however, Erie and its creeks still remain popular for fishing enthusiasts.

A cultural landmark since the 1950s, West Erie Plaza flourished until its decline in the late 1990s with the closing of the West Erie Plaza Theater. In 2012, VCG Properties purchased the plaza for the purpose of redevelopment, which began in 2015. Since then, new life has been invigorated into the plaza, including new stores and restaurants. Since the 1960s, the landscape surrounding the plaza has become virtually unrecognizable due to urban redevelopment.

Post-1960s photograph of Holland and East Seventh Streets. In the distance is the old Muffler King building. *Erie County Historical Society.*

The duplex at 717 Holland Street had been witness to the disastrous 1915 Millcreek flood that tore through the area, causing millions in damage. The brick building that housed Muffler King stood on the corner of East Eighth and Holland Streets, playing host to numerous auto-related businesses until it was demolished in 2022, along with the old Hill Mill Dairy building, after Erie Insurance purchased the land as part of the company's plan to rehabilitate blight in nearby East Side neighborhoods.

The corner of East Eighth and Holland Streets is full of beautiful green grass, fluttering in the morning breeze, the air calm and peaceful, with many unaware of its dark history.

Ax Murder Hollow has also fallen victim to urban development since 1963. The legend of Ax Murder Hollow, however, remains popular among local teenagers and the morbidly curious searching for a scare, many of them unaware of the true tragedy associated with the hollow.

The investigations that took place between 1960 and 1963 into the attacks against women in Erie affected more lives than we will probably ever know. Leonard Meucci was a broken man after his wife's death and passed in 1965 at the age of eighty. All of Laura Mutch's children have since passed away; however, grandchildren and great-grandchildren of Laura still are told stories of their grandmother and how her life was tragically cut short, a reminder of how painful her death is, almost sixty-two years later.

Charlotte Mossburg never returned to Erie. Following her husband's death in 1977, she remained a devoted mother to her children. A member of Saybrook United Methodist Church, Mossburg spent her time crocheting for children and friends, baking, making chocolate candy and watching soap operas. Finding Laura Mutch's body haunted her for the rest of her life until her passing in 2009 at the age of eighty-six in Ashtabula, Ohio.

Sophie Gorchinsky passed away in 1992 at the age of seventy-seven. Ann Kopes retired from the Erie Universal Company in 1980 after working there for fifteen years. A member of the Lakefront Senior Citizens Club and the Siebenbuerger Lady Bowlers Club, Kopes died in 1984 at the age of sixty-nine.

Irene Fogle worked at General Electric as a machine operator and was a member of the Pulaski Club. Known for her love of traveling and playing bingo, Fogle moved with her husband, John Osborne, to Oklahoma after her retirement in 1997. She died the following year at the age of sixty.

The Reverend Richard J. Gibbons became the founder of the Jamestown Revival Center in Jamestown, New York, and remained well known in Jamestown. Gibbons traveled with a worldwide ministry, preaching the gospel, until his reunion with his deceased wife and son when he passed away in 2020 at the age of ninety.

The saga of Erie's Backyard Strangler saw the involvement of some of the area's most influential reporters and journalists, who broadcast the story through television screens, radios and newspapers.

During Hyle Vance Richmond's career with WICU, the station became the highest rated in Erie. Anchoring alongside Richmond were Ned McGrath, Shirley Ramsey, Bill Knupp and Vance McBryde. Richmond remained highly respected for the rest of his career as a broadcast journalist and, following his retirement, traveled the world with his wife, Caliope, doting on their children and grandchildren. They lived in Florida and Arizona before Caliope's passing in 2013. Afterward, Richmond moved to Omaha, Nebraska, to be closer to family. He passed away in 2017 at the age of ninety.

The National Legal Aid and Defender Association awarded Garth Minegar and a fellow reporter the Emery A. Brownell award in 1965 for articles and editorials that led to the establishment of Erie County's public defender's office. Following this, Minegar was a city editor for twenty-five years before becoming the managing editor for the *Evening Sentinel* in Ansonia, Connecticut, until its closing in 1991. Despite contracting postpolio syndrome in 1985, Minegar worked until he was advised to retire in 1996. Garth Minegar passed away at the age of sixty-eight in 2002.

Tom McCormack left the *Erie Morning News* to work for Eastman Kodak as a publications editor. Following his retirement, McCormack became one of the founding members of the Upstate New York Chapter of the Toy Train Collectors Society and enjoyed spending time with his family, especially his children and grandchildren, until his passing in Henrietta, New York, in 2005 at the age of seventy-two.

George Frazier continued to write about sports, jazz, politics and daily life and, in 1970, joined the *Boston Globe* as a columnist writing four times a week. Frazier succumbed to lung cancer in 1974 at the age of sixty-three in Cambridge, Massachusetts. To this day, Frazier is still heralded as one of Boston's best journalists.

It was the police who endured the massive investigations into Erie's Backyard Strangler and other attacks throughout the 1960s, and without today's technological advances in forensics, they were often faced with insurmountable odds and frustration.

Armand Chimenti became instrumental in founding Erie's canine unit and the city's traffic court in the 1960s. After five years of leading the police department as chief, Chimenti retired in 1971 at the age of fifty-five.

"He's done more for the police department than anybody," Mayor Louis J. Tullio told reporters. "The toughest job in the city, you know, is running the police department."

Chimenti and Deputy Police Chief Mario S. Bagnoni, who had also retired, were honored at a dinner held by the Sons of Italy Lodge 921 on January 25, 1971, for "dedicated and outstanding service to the city."

In the late 1970s, Chimenti returned to police work, serving as county detective for four years. Chimenti was widely mourned in 1985 when he passed away at the age of sixty-nine.

Lieutenant Philip Lupo served twenty-nine years with the police and was president of the Fraternal Order of Police when he died suddenly on July 29, 1973, at the age of sixty-five. Lillian Strand continued to proudly serve the community and retired from the Erie City Police Department in 1988. She passed away in 2015 at the age of ninety-one.

Frank Figaski furthered his education at Gannon University and practiced as a substitute teacher at Strong Vincent High School in the fall of 1962. Figaski later became an elementary school teacher for fifteen years with the Erie School District. When he passed away in 1991, Figaski was still fondly remembered and respected throughout Erie.

Chester A. Wizikowski remained a colorful figure in Erie's history after his resignation from the police department in April 1965, following being laid off for a year after sustaining injuries in a car accident while on duty. The following month, Wizikowski announced and ran a successful campaign for alderman of the Second Ward.

Just after midnight on February 20, 1967, Wizikowski found himself arguing with fellow alderman and political foe Michael Kinecki inside the Polish Foresters Club. As Kinecki left the club, Wizikowski assaulted him. When firemen arrived, they found Kinecki lying on the ground bleeding from the face and having difficulty breathing.

Wizikowski was charged with aggravated assault and battery but never faced jail time for the incident. Into the 1970s, he attempted to run again for Second Ward alderman but was defeated. Wizikowski died in Erie in 2001 at the age of eighty-seven.

Raymond J. Lapenz remained with the Erie City Police Department until his resignation in 1971 and later worked for the Veterans Affairs Medical Center in Erie. Following his retirement, Lapenz enjoyed landscaping and golf and cherished his time working with Little League Baseball in Erie. Lapenz passed away on August 3, 2022, while this book was being written, and was one of the last detectives alive who worked on the Backyard Strangler investigation.

Robert J. Ross remained a detective until his retirement in 1968, having served for twenty-seven years. He passed away in November 1983 at the age of seventy-four. Maurice J. Sheehan retired in 1965 after serving twenty-two years with the department and passed away in May 1984 at the age of seventy-four.

In July 1987, Lieutenant Carl Kalinowski was forced to retire based on a 1971 city ordinance requiring mandatory retirement at the age of sixty-five for police and firefighters.

"As far as I'm concerned, I'm not leaving until I see something in writing," Kalinowski protested. Kalinowski's protest, along with that of then–deputy chief Alfonse Natalie, set off a confrontation with local officials. Mayor Louis J. Tullio announced that he would be willing to compromise with the officers to work through November 1, after city council voted, in a 4–1 majority, to retain both men.

While Kalinowski was convinced he was still capable of carrying out his duties, Erie County judge George Levin ruled Tullio's administration could force both men into mandatory retirement, and Kalinowski was told he needed to retire by October 5 of that year. After thirty-seven years of service, Kalinowski's forced departure left a sour taste in his mouth, and he filed a grievance against the city. In his spare time, Kalinowski enjoyed working in his garden and spending time with his grandchildren.

Kalinowski passed away in 2011 in Erie.

Thomas J. Stanton attained the rank of captain in charge of the detective bureau, a role he held for several years before retirement. Appointed second deputy for the Erie County coroner in February 1986, Stanton suffered a heart attack at the age of fifty-five several months later. Stanton was well liked and respected, and his death came as a shock to those in Erie.

Mike Snider retired from the Erie City Police Department in 1969 after twenty-two years of service. Following a series of intestinal diseases and heart issues, Snider died in 1983 at the young age of fifty-nine in Buffalo, New York. "Mike had a soft touch for the bums, the guys who were down on their luck," recalled his partner, Charles McCurdy. "He was always good hearted."

McCurdy, then a captain, paid a final tribute to his friend by being one of the pallbearers at his funeral.

McCurdy reached the rank of deputy chief and retired after thirty-three years of service. An avid fisherman and hunter, he enjoyed spending time with his children and grandchildren. He passed away at the age of eighty-seven in May 2012.

Ed Pianka became a detective sergeant with the police department until his death in May 1992 at the age of sixty-four. Melvin Swanson remained a detective sergeant until his retirement in 1971. Swanson died in Erie in 2003 at the age of eighty-two.

Captain Paul J. DeDionisio retired after thirty years of service with the department, becoming chief county detective for the district attorney's office, a position he held until the age of seventy. A member of Sacred Heart Church, DeDionisio enjoyed horse racing, playing pinochle and spending time with his brothers and sons at hunting camp. A devoted Yankees fan, DeDionisio regarded his greatest blessings as being his wife, Mary, and his children, grandchildren and great-grandchildren.

Paul J. DeDionisio died at the age of ninety-six in 2009.

Former chief Edward Williams passed away unexpectedly at the age of fifty-nine in 1968. His successor, George Radaker, served as chief until his 1966, when Armand Chimenti was promoted by Mayor Tullio. Reminiscing about his time as chief, Radaker said, "It has been, indeed, a pleasure to have been associated with the City of Erie and its fine personnel for more than 24 years." George Radaker died at the age of sixty-three in 1972.

Deputy Chief Chester J. Miller retired from the Erie City Police Department in 1968 after serving for twenty-six years. Following his retirement, in 1970,

Miller was appointed by Coroner Merle Wood as his deputy but suffered a heart attack at his home several days later at the age of fifty-nine.

Edward Strong passed away at the age of eighty-two in Lawrence Park.

William Serafini retired in 1972 after serving thirty years with the Erie City Police Department. A founder of the Police Athletic League and an officer in the Sons of Italy, Serafini spent his time after retirement gardening. Serafini died in 1999 at the age of eighty-nine.

Merle E. Wood served as coroner until 2000, ending a forty-year career investigating more than seventeen thousand deaths in addition to directing the Wood Funeral Home. Wood recalled many devastating memories as coroner, none more so than assisting with the aftermath of the deadly tornadoes that struck Albion and Cranesville in 1985. Following retirement, Wood looked forward to spending more time with family, golfing, bowling and traveling with his wife, Phoebe.

Wood continues to enjoy his time in retirement.

John A. Fust remained a pathologist for Hamot Hospital and eventually retired to Mayville, New York, where he remained a devoted parishioner at St. Paul's Episcopal Church. Dr. Fust passed away in Erie in 2017 at the age of ninety-six.

After his tenure as president judge of the Orphans Court of Erie County, Herbert Johnson Jr. returned to practicing private law in Erie, joining the Elderkin, Martin, Kelly and Massina firm in 2007. Johnson was serving as vice-chancellor of the Episcopal Diocese of Northwest Pennsylvania at the time of his death in 2008 at the age of ninety-two.

Richard Scarpitti served as a special deputy attorney general until 1972. A chairman of the Erie Chapter of the Pennsylvania Trial Lawyers Association, Scarpitti was also a member of local organizations such as the Zem Zem Temple Shrine, the Kahkwa Club and the Board of the International Institute. Scarpitti passed away in 1984 at the age of fifty-seven.

Richard Brabender would go on to serve as Erie County solicitor. In 1972, he opened Brabender Southwoods Golf Course in McKean. Brabender passed away in 2011 at the age of eighty-eight.

Dr. Frank J. Pizzat served thirty-nine years in the clinical psychology field and was a consultant to the Sarah Reed Children's Center, Harborcreek Youth Services, Erie County Probation Offices and Office of Children and Youth. Affiliated with Gannon University for twenty-five years, Pizzat served as director of psychological services and associate professor in the graduate counseling program. Dr. Pizzat passed away in 1991 at the age of sixty-seven.

Dr. Michael F. Cleary left Erie to head the psychiatric division at John Peter Smith in Fort Worth, Texas, followed by a move to Arizona, where he became a psychiatric consultant to state and federal courts, working closely with the Department of Corrections and Indian Medical Service before retiring in 2017 at the age of ninety. A passionate golfer and lover of books and opera, Dr. Cleary cherished his family and was known for his generosity and compassion. Dr. Cleary passed away in 2019 at the age of ninety-two in Scottsdale, Arizona.

Helen Knost remained in Erie. A devoted member of the Erie Church of Christ, she was also an avid member of the Presque Isle Travelers RV Club with her husband, Richard. Survived by her four children and her husband, Helen died in 1998.

District Attorney Edward H. Carney presented the Knost case to a grand jury on Monday, April 27, 1964, in part because the statute of limitations of two years was steadfastly approaching. Helen appeared and testified, recounting her horrific experience. The panel returned an indictment the following day against "John Doe" for the attack, keeping the charge of intent to kill open indefinitely. It remains an active indictment to this day. The identity of Helen Knost's attacker has never been confirmed, and the case remains open with the Pennsylvania State Police.

Daniel Roy Biebighauser filed a motion for a new trial through his attorneys in 1970, seven years after his conviction. In his petition, Biebighauser claimed his car and home were unconstitutionally searched by police and his confession was coerced and infringed on his privilege against self-incrimination. Biebighauser's appeal was denied by the Erie County courts the following year, and in 1973, the Pennsylvania Supreme Court upheld his conviction. This did not deter Biebighauser from attempting to request parole the same year, something he continued to do into the 1980s.

"Please do all in your power to keep her murderer, Biebighauser, in jail," Crotty's aunt wrote to the Pennsylvania Board of Pardons in 1987. "We all died a little when Lynn left us. They have not forgotten this tragedy. He will kill again if he gets out."

Biebighauser remained incarcerated for the rest of his life, and in a form of poetic justice, he died from brain cancer on March 22, 2007, at the Pennsylvania State Correctional Facility in Laurel Highlands.

In the series of attacks that occurred between 1960 and 1964, Biebighauser was only connected to the murder of Lynn Crotty and the assault on Nancy Wierzbicki.

Biebighauser is documented as having moved back to Erie in February 1962. This does not negate his importance as a suspect in the attack on Clara Carrig, as it cannot be confirmed if he was present in Erie at the time, especially since he was known to use his leave time to visit Erie, which could coordinate with some of the attacks. A thorough search of additional military records could be performed to confirm this, but such a search has not been performed as of this writing.

Based on Biebighauser's background, including his murder of an animal and setting fires at an early age, coupled with the lack of a father figure and a domineering mother, one can only wonder, with a sense of enigmatic fright, what else Biebighauser was involved in that will likely remain forever unknown.

Nancy Wierzbicki, Biebighauser's teenage victim, later married twice and had children of her own. She still resides in Erie. Her brave testimony provided at Biebighauser's trial helped shed light on one of Erie's most infamous murderers. As a survivor, in a day and age when victims of sexual assault are being heard, Nancy's story should never be forgotten.

John Floyd Harvey stayed out of the public eye following the murder of Lynn Crotty. Still alive, he is last known to have resided in Harborcreek Township.

Paulette Cywinski later left the area, married and had a family of her own. After the death of her husband in 1984, she remarried and now lives in Alaska, running a successful rental business.

Detective Sergeant Leo Weir retired in 1966 and became deputy coroner for Erie County for two years under Coroner Merle Wood. Weir served two terms as Erie County commissioner and worked in the public relations department for Northwest Engineering for seven years. An active member of the Lakewood United Methodist Church, Weir remained involved in dozens of local clubs and organizations, including the *Erie Daily Times* Old Newsies, before passing away in 2002.

After serving thirty-seven years with the Pennsylvania State Police, Lewis Penman focused on his family. He continued his passion for gardening, woodworking, collecting railroad antiques and camping until his passing in 2007 at the age of eighty-eight.

Detective Tyco Lange retired from the state police in 1974 and became a crossing guard for Lord Corporation. A member of the American Legion Millcreek Post 733 and Cascade Club, he passed away in 1991 in Erie.

Clara Carrig remained in Erie with her husband, Thomas. After his passing in 1966, she spent the remainder of her life in a local nursing home before passing away in 1978 at the age of eighty-nine.

Despite numerous attempts to locate Clara's attacker, her case remains open with the Erie City Police Department.

Clifford Salow was never charged in the murder of Eleanor Free.

In February 2001, Erie County district attorney Brad Foulk reopened the investigation into Free's murder. All case reports, along with extensive evidence, were retrieved for review. The review, Foulk claimed, was due to a tip received from an unnamed individual.

Salow died on October 22, 2001, at the age of eighty-four. Following his passing, the district attorney's office confirmed that it had cleared the case, with local law enforcement satisfied Salow was responsible for the crime and could no longer be prosecuted.

Lawyers and judges involved in these cases from 1960 to 1963 fought an ever-changing battle on the landscape of law during a decade that would change America, evident from Willman's convictions in both 1964 and 1968.

Burton R. Laub became the fourth dean of Dickinson School of Law in 1966, serving until September 1974. Laub remained active in the law community and authored many legal works while also spending his time working as an artist; his artwork appeared in the 1984 sesquicentennial edition of *The Dickinson School of Law—Proud and Independent*. In 1983, a classroom at Dickinson was dedicated in his honor. Judge Laub passed away in 1999 at the age of ninety-six.

Judge Elmer L. Evans retired in January 1970. "He was understanding, very understanding of people," Judge William E. Pfadt remembered. "And his decisions were always very human." Judge Evans passed away on October 1, 1974, at the age of eighty-two. Following his death, Evans and past Erie County Court judges who were deceased were honored during the dedication of the new jail and the $6.3 million addition to the Erie County Courthouse.

Judge Lindley R. McClelland remained a judge with the Erie County Court of Common Pleas until his retirement in 1981. Following his retirement, he bravely fought cancer until his death in 1991 at the age of seventy-five. The *Erie Daily Times* remembered McClelland "did more than look the part, he lived it to the fullest, committing himself wholly to what is, after all, the most awesomely responsible of all local government positions."

Michael Kinecki served the Second Ward for twenty years in his capacity as alderman. A member of St. Stanislaus Church and founding president of the Holy Name Society, Kinecki was a lifelong member of the Foresters Beneficial Association, the Polish Sharpshooters, the Moniuszko Singing Society and the Huzar Club. Kinecki passed away in 1981 at the age of sixty-four.

Bernard F. Quinn practiced law for many years at the Quinn law firm while in Erie. In 1972, he formed Quinn Enterprises with his eldest son, overseeing several McDonald's restaurant franchises in Willingboro, New Jersey. Quinn passed away at the age of seventy-five in Sun City, Arizona, in 1993.

Edward H. Carney remained an Erie County common pleas judge until his retirement in 1981. In 1973, Carney gained national attention when he was chosen by the Pennsylvania Supreme Court to preside over the trial of conspirators charged in the 1969 New Year's Eve murders of United Mine Workers dissident Joseph A. "Jock" Yablonski and his wife and daughter. Eight conspirators, including UMW president W.A. "Tony" Boyle, either were convicted or pleaded guilty.

In 1975, Carney presided over the trial of Donald Lee Chism, who murdered his wife, his three children, his wife's uncle and his adoptive stepfather. The sensational trial was moved to Williamsport, Pennsylvania, and resulted in Chism's conviction. Carney's tenure as judge saw him preside over more than four hundred criminal and three hundred civil trials. Judge Carney passed away at the age of eighty-five in 1998.

Dana Sherwood Jones served as a public defender until 1970. Jones became the first full-time solicitor for the City of Erie school district until 1973, when he returned to the role of public defender until 1975 and then became a juvenile court prosecutor until 1990. When he passed away in 2011 at the age of ninety, Jones was remembered for his involvement in numerous charities and associations throughout Erie.

James E. Beveridge continued to practice law privately in Erie for twenty-five years and served as a solicitor for the County of Erie and Office of Children and Youth. Beveridge passed away in 2016 at the age of eighty-three.

Will J. Schaaf remained a partner with the law firm Marsh, Spaeder, Bauer, Spaeder & Shaaf and served as president and chancellor of the Erie County Bar Association. Schaaf passed away at his residence in 2011 at the age of ninety-two.

Vedder J. White served as a public defender in Erie County for a total of seven years. "His role as a lawyer was to help people," friend and local attorney Joseph Messina told the *Erie Daily Times*. "He was a champion of the underdog." Following his departure from the public defender's office, White became an active bankruptcy practitioner and member of the Bankruptcy Trustee Panel. In the 1980s, White joined Elderkin, Martin, Kelly and Messina, becoming a partner on January 1, 1993.

Unknown to many, White was undergoing dialysis treatments for kidney problems. The illness never stopped White. "We spent time with him on several occasions on the golf course," *Erie Times News* columnist Ed Matthews wrote in his column. "Vedder was a very fine man, very popular with his many clients as well as other lawyers."

White underwent a liver and kidney transplant in 1993 but passed away several days later at the age of fifty-two at Presbyterian University Hospital in Pittsburgh. His death stunned members of the Erie County Bar Association and those within the Erie community.

Michael Palmisano served as an assistant district attorney under District Attorney William Pfadt until 1972. After a brief hiatus, Palmisano returned to the district attorney's office from 1976 to 1979 under District Attorney Robert Chase before returning to private practice in 1980, where he handled both civil and criminal cases. Palmisano was appointed by then–county executive Judy Lynch as a public defender in 1988, the same year he unsuccessfully ran for Erie County judge.

Palmisano remained with the public defender's office until 1998, when he was nominated by Pennsylvania governor Tom Ridge to be Erie County's next judge, taking the position of Michael T. Joyce when he was elected to the state superior court. Palmisano has since retired and remains in Erie.

The multiple investigations that occurred between 1960 and 1964 introduced Erie to infamous individuals of the time, in stories ranging from the bizarre to the macabre.

Following his arson spree, Richard Worlund was sent to Warren State Hospital for commitment and psychiatric observation. Not much more is known about him, and following his release, he moved out west to California, where he died in 2003.

Former Erie resident James Robert Moore, New York state's longest serving inmate, was granted parole in 2022 by the New York parole board. He was released in June 2022 and resides in Cayuga County, New York, with his wife.

Ralph William Rogers was indicted on May 1, 1964, and scheduled for trial in September 1964. Prior to the trial, both prosecution and defense attorneys sparred over the evidence and Rogers's confessions. Just as jurors were being selected, Rogers surprised those in the courtroom when he pleaded guilty on the morning of September 23, 1964.

Rogers was found guilty of second-degree murder on February 8, 1965, and sentenced to eight to twenty years in the Western Penitentiary. Rogers later sought to have his case remanded back to county court in 1968, claiming he was not informed of his right to counsel on appeal and that the use of his statement was illegal because he invoked his Fifth Amendment rights.

The Pennsylvania Supreme Court denied Rogers's appeal in October 1970.

After serving seven and a half years of his sentence, Rogers was released from the Western Penitentiary as part of a pilot program coordinated by the Allegheny Community College, working with the Allegheny County Jail. One of six inmates released in the summer of 1970, Rogers had recently finished earning an associate degree in business administration, with one of the stipulations of his release being that he continue his schooling.

On November 28, 1971, Rogers was arrested in Wilkinsburg, Pennsylvania, on charges of assault and battery with the intent to rape or maim. The following day, his body was found by a prison guard in his cell, having strangled himself with one of the chains that suspended his cot from the wall.

As for John Howard Willman, nothing in his background prior to 1960 indicates that he was responsible for any other attacks on women in the Erie area. An exhaustive search, utilizing what records are available, confirmed that while serving with the national guard, Willman never presented any disciplinary issues. There is also no indication Willman attacked other women at any point in his life. This is pure conjecture, however. As attacks and assaults are not always reported, it is difficult to say when, or if, Willman attacked or murdered any other women.

There are still several troubling factors in the case against Willman. These include the lack of physical evidence tying Willman to the murder scene at 717 Holland Street. And then there is the testimony from family members who confirm that on the night of December 30, 1960, Willman went to bed early and never left the home.

The difficulty in locating witnesses who could place Willman at Huck's Café on the night of the murder also presents its own issues. What we are left with are John Willman's statements, which implicate himself in the murder. These statements and confessions, however, are not without scrutiny. Many of the details Willman provided in his statements had already been made public. And if we are to believe Willman was, as Lucille Koch testified, an acquaintance of the Mutch family, there is the chance he knew information about Laura that the general public was unaware of. These are just some of the numerous questions that have never been answered.

One has to wonder: if the possibility exists that Willman was truly responsible for the murder of Laura Mutch, what else he was responsible for that we do not know about? That is not to suggest Willman was not capable of murdering Laura Mutch.

The assault on Davida Boyer, as well as similar attacks in the area, indicate a blitz-style series of attacks by the individual responsible. The assault of Boyer also showed Willman's ability to attack and subdue a potential victim. Coupled with the 1956 arrest for indecent exposure, when Willman was arrested in Lawrence Park wearing women's underwear, these are clues that someday could shed further light on Willman's life and potential criminal propensities.

The fact that John Howard Willman, Daniel Roy Biebighauser and Ralph William Rogers were all convicted for similar crimes during a period when more than fifteen known women were attacked or assaulted, with those responsible unknown, is truly frightening.

Despite the numerous questions, this does not entirely negate the belief that justice has not been served.

John Howard Willman served the remainder of his sentence and was released and returned to Erie, where he resided with his siblings. He never again committed any known offenses, and on August 12, 2013, at a retirement home in Erie, he passed away at the age of eighty-six.

Following his death, Willman was buried with full military honors in Lakeside Cemetery. He was buried next to his siblings, and his grave is unadorned, save for its bronze grave marker. In a measure of unknown fate, several hundred yards south, one can locate the headstone for Laura Mutch.

APPENDIX

THE STATEMENTS OF
JOHN HOWARD WILLMAN

T he following statements were obtained from John Howard Willman between July 13, 1963, and August 31, 1963.

These statements were instrumental for the prosecution during trials in 1964 and 1968, forming the basis of the case against Willman. Obtained from the original court transcripts when entered into evidence, Willman's statements are reproduced here, to the public, for the first time.

The following four pages contain Willman's first statement, obtained by detectives on July 13, 1963, regarding the attack on Davida Boyer, taken at the detective bureau of the City of Erie Police Department.

McCurdy

1	A	No, no force.
2	Q	Was he coerced in any way?
3	A	No.
4	Q	Were there any promises made if he would give you this
5		statement?
6	A	No, there's no promises made. As a matter of fact,
7		that's one of the questions in the statement.
8	Q	Was he threatened in any way?
9	A	No.
10	Q	Would you say that this statement is a free and voluntary
11		statement of Mr. Willman?
12	A	Yes, I would.
13	Q	Officer, will you read the statement?
14		MR. QUINN: Can we ask another
15		question?
16		THE COURT: Yes.
17		BY MR. QUINN:
18	Q	Was he told that if he didn't sign the statement he would
19		be given the electric chair or sent to North Warren?
20	A	No, sir, he was not. He was never told that.
21		MR. QUINN: That's all.
22		BY MR. CARNEY:
23	Q	Read the statement?
24	A	"Statement of John H. Willman, aged thirty-six, truck
25		driver, 452 East Eighth Street. Taken at Detective Bureau,

McCurdy

1   "Erie Police Department, Erie, Pennsylvania, at 11:50 PM

2   July 13th, 1963, by Captain Carl Kalinowski, of the Erie

3   Police Department, in the presence of Detective Sergeant

4   Charles McCurdy, also of the Erie Police Department.

5   Q. What is your name?

6   A. John H. Willman.

7   Q. Where do you live?

8   A. 452 East Eighth Street.

9   Q. How old are you?

10   A. Thirty-six years old.

11   Q. Can you read and write?

12   A. I can read but I'm not too good at writing.

13   Q. Are you willing to make a statement of what you know

14   about the assault on Davida Logan Boyer about 3:00 AM on

15   July 6th, 1963, on East Front Street between Holland and

16   German Street?

17   A. Yes.

18   Q. After I have explained to you that anything you say

19   here can and will be used against you should this case

20   come up in a court of law at a later date, are you still

21   willing to make this statement?

22   A. Yes.

23   Q. Now, John H. Willman, in your own words explain to me

24   just what took place?

25   A. I went to the Tally-Ho Bar at 18th and State Street

McCurdy

1   " about six-thirty PM on Friday July 5th, 1963. I then

2   started to drink beer. I was alone. After I was there a

3   while I met a stock-car driver from Busti, New York, and

4   we had a few beers. I then offered to buy a lady a drink.

5   She accepted. After I bought her a drink we sat down in

6   a booth. I then bought her some more drinks and we then

7   danced a few times. The lady asked me for a ride home

8   and I told her that I would give her a ride home. I had

9   the truck of my employer, the Benacci Produce Company,

10   parked by the Tally-Ho Bar. She got in the truck and I

11   then drove down towards the lake. We parked there and she

12   tried to get out of the door and I pulled her back. We

13   both fell out of the cab. Her glasses fell from her face

14   and her teeth came out of her mouth. And I fell on top of

15   her. The lady ran to a house, before she left she told

16   me to get out of here. I got home way (home some way),

17   but I don't remember how.

18   Q. Is this statement of two pages the truth?

19   A. Yes.

20   Q. John, I show you a green visor cap. Is this your cap?

21   A. Yes.

22   Q. How have you been treated since your arrest?

23   A. Good. "

24   At the bottom of this page it is sworn to by Michael J.

25   Kinecki on the 14th of July, 1963.

IMELDA BOWES   48

McCurdy

1   "Continued statement of John H. Willman, age thirty-six,

2   truck driver, taken at the Detective Bureau, Erie Police

3   Department, Erie, Pennsylvania, at 11:50 PM., July 13th,

4   1963, by Captain Carl Kalinowski.

5   Q. Have you made this two-page statement of your own

6   free will, without the use of force, fear, threats or

7   promises?

8   A. Yes.

9   Q. Have you read this statement before signing it?

10 A. Yes.", in the defendant's own handwriting.

11 "Signature, John H. Willman.

12 Witnesses: Captain Carl Kalinowski and Detective Sergeant

13 Charles McCurdy." And this page is also sworn to before

14 Alderman Michael J. Kinecki.

15   BY MR. CARNEY:

16 Q   Now, Officer, on page one I notice the signature is written

17   across the face of the page, and ask you whose signature

18   that is?

19 A   That's John Willman's signature.

20 Q   Were you present when that signature was made?

21 A   Yes.

22 Q   On the top of the page I notice some initials. Can you

23   tell us whose initials they are?

24 A   That's John H. Willman's. We typed "152 East 8th St." for

25   the address. and we had him correct it to "452". It was

The following four pages contain Willman's second statement, obtained by detectives on July 14, 1963, regarding the Laura Mutch murder, taken at the detective bureau of the City of Erie Police Department.

McCurdy

1	MR. CARNEY: At this time I offer
2	Exhibit 15 into evidence.
3	MR. QUINN: We object to it for the
4	reasons--the same objection we had before.
5	THE COURT: We understand it is under
6	the same objection, and it is admitted.
7	BY MR. CARNEY:
8	Q Will you read the exhibit?
9	A "Statement of John Willman, age thirty-six, truck driver,
10	of 452 East 8th Street, taken at the Bureau of Criminal
11	Investigation, Erie Police Department, Erie, Pennsylvania,
12	at 11:30 P.M., July 14th, 1963, by Detective Sergeant
13	Charles McCurdy of the Erie Police Department, in the
14	presence of Detective Sergeant Melvin Swanson, also of
15	the Erie Police Department.
16	Q. What is your name?
17	A. John Howard Willman.
18	Q. Where do you live?
19	A. 452 East 8th Street.
20	Q. Can you read and write?
21	A. Yes.
22	Q. How old are you?
23	A. Thirty-six.
24	Q. Are you willing to make a statement of what you know
25	about the murder of Laura Mutch that took place December

McCurdy

1	"30th, 1960, at 717 Holland Street in the city of Erie,
2	Pennsylvania?
3	A. Yes.
4	Q. After I have explained to you that anything you say
5	here can and will be used against you should this case
6	come up in a court of law at a later date, are you still
7	willing to make this statement?
8	A. Yes.
9	Q. Now, John H. Willman, in your own words explain to me
10	just what took place.
11	A. I think I was at Huck's drinking. From there I walked
12	and met this woman, Mrs. Mutch. And then we walked, and
13	she didn't tell me where she lived. And then we came to
14	this house. And then we went between the buildings to
15	the back yard. Then she fell on the ice and her scarf
16	fell off. I then grabbed her and put the scarf in her
17	mouth so she wouldn't struggle. Then she was unconscious.
18	And then I pulled down her stockings, and pulled down her
19	pants. Then I screwed her. I then pulled the scarf out
20	of her mouth. Then I went home.
21	Q. John, what did you do with the scarf after you took
22	it out of her mouth?
23	A. Put it in the yard.
24	Q. John, how do you know this lady that you left in the
25	yard at the rear of 717 Holland Street was Mrs. Laura Mutch?

McCurdy

1 "A. I read it in the paper the next day.

2 Q. John, would you say that Mrs. Mutch was an older

3 woman or a young girl?

4 A. I would say an older woman.

5 Q. Would you say that she was thirty years old or fifty

6 years old?

7 A. Fifty.

8 Q. John, why are you telling us about this murder now?

9 A. Because it was on my mind.

10 Q. Why didn't you tell the police about it the next day

11 when you read about it in the paper?

12 A. Because I was scared."

13 "Page two. Continued statement of John Howard Willman,

14 age thirty-six, truck driver, taken at the Bureau of

15 Criminal Investigation, Erie Police Department, Erie,

16 Pennsylvania, at eleven-thirty P.M., July 14th, 1963, by

17 Detective Sergeant Charles A. McCurdy, in the presence of

18 Detective Sergeant Melvin Swanson, also of the Erie Police

19 Department.

20 Q. John, did you know that Laura Mutch was dead when you

21 left the yard?

22 A. No.

23 Q. John, are you sure that you are telling the truth and

24 not making this story up?

25 A. Yes, I am telling the truth.

McCurdy

1   "Q. John, did this woman have a Bible?

2   A. Yes.

3   Q. John, what did you and Laura Mutch talk about when you

4   walked with her?

5   A. She talked about religion.

6   Q. John, do you remember passing any people on the street

7   when you walked with Laura Mutch?

8   A. No, I don't remember passing any people on the street.

9   Q. John did you at any time hear a dog barking?

10   A. Yes.

11   Q. Was this after you and Laura Mutch was in the back yard

12   at 717 Holland that you heard this dog barking?

13   A. Yes.

14   Q. Is this statement of two pages the truth?

15   A. Yes.

16   Q. How have you been treated since your arrest?

17   A. Good.

18   Q. Have you made this two page statement of your own

19   free will, without the use of force, fear, threats or

20   promises?

21   A. Yes.

22   Q. Have you read this statement before signing it?"

23   A. In the defendant's own handwriting, "Yes".

24   "Signature, John H. Willman. Witnesses, Detective Sergeant

25   Melvin Swanson, Detective Sergeant Charles McCurdy."

The following four pages contain Willman's third statement, obtained by detectives on August 31, 1963, regarding the Laura Mutch murder, taken at the Erie County Prison.

McCurdy

1	A	I have no way of knowing where he would be in the County
2		Jail. That would be up to the warden, Bruce Reeder,
3		where they would put a man in the County Jail. I have
4		no knowledge of that.
5	Q	Did Mr. Reeder know he was under suspicion of murder at
6		that time?
7	A	I have no way of knowing what Mr. Reeder knows.
8		MR. QUINN: That's all we have.
9		MR. CARNEY: At this time I will
10		offer Commonwealth's Exhibit 16 into evidence.
11		MR. QUINN: Same objection.
12		THE COURT: It is admitted under the
13		objection.
14		BY MR. CARNEY:
15	Q	Officer, will you read the statement into evidence?
16	A	"August 31st, 1963. Statement of John Howard Willman, age
17		thirty-six, truck driver, 452 East 8th Street, taken at
18		the Erie County Prison, Erie, Pennsylvania, at 10:00 A.M.,
19		August 31st, 1963, by Detective Sergeant Charles McCurdy
20		of the Erie Police Department, in the presence of Detective
21		Sergeant Michael Snider, also of the Erie Police Department.
22		Q. What is your name?
23		A. John Howard Willman.
24		Q. Where do you live?
25		A. 452 East 8th Street.

IMELDA BOWES

106

McCurdy

1   "Q.   Can you read and write?

2   A.   Yes.

3   Q.   How old are you?

4   A.   Thirty-six.

5   Q.   Are you willing to make a statement of what you know

6   about the murder of Laura Mutch that took place December

7   30th, 1960, at 717 Holland Street in the city of Erie,

8   Pennsylvania?

9   A.   Yes.

10   Q.   After I have explained to you that anything you say

11   here can and will be used against you should this case

12   come up in a court of law at a later date, are you still

13   willing to make this statement?

14   A.   Yes.

15   Q.   Now, John H. Willman, in your own words, explain to

16   me just what took place?

17   A.   I was drinking at Huck's place. Then I started to

18   walk home. I then met this woman, Mrs. Mutch. She passed

19   me as I was walking home. I then followed her, and she

20   talked to me. She talked about religion. Then she said

21   she wanted someone to walk her home. She didn't tell me

22   where she lived. Then we walked and we came to this house.

23   Then we went in between the building to the back yard. She

24   fell on the ice. I then went down on my knees. I then

25   put this scarf in her mouth, so she couldn't breathe.

McCurdy

1   "I then pulled down her pants and screwed her. Then I

2   went home.

3   Q. How do you know this woman that you left in the yard,

4   at 717 Holland Street, was Laura Mutch?

5   A. I don't remember.

6   Q. John, would you say that Mrs. Mutch was an older woman

7   or a young girl?

8   A. Older woman.

9   Q. Would you say that she was thirty years old or fifty

10 years old?

11 A. Fifty years old.

12 Q. Why are you telling us about this murder now?

13 A. It's on my mind.

14 Q. Why didn't you tell the police about it the next day?

15 A. I was scared."

16 "Page two. Continued statement of John Howard Willman,

17   age thirty-six, truck driver, taken at the Erie County

18   Prison, at 10:00 A.M., August 31st, 1963, by Detective

19   Sergeant Charles A. McCurdy of the Erie Police Department,

20   in the presence of Detective Sergeant Michael Snider,

21   also of the Erie Police Department.

22   Q. Did you know that Laura Mutch was dead when you left

23   her in the yard?

24   A. No.

25   Q. Are you sure that you are telling the truth and not

McCurdy

1   "making this story up?

2   A. Yes.

3   Q. Did this woman have a Bible?

4   A. Yes.

5   Q. Do you remember passing any people on the street when

6   you walked with Laura Mutch?

7   A. No.

8   Q. Did you at any time hear a dog barking?

9   A. Yes.

10 Q. Where did you hear this dog barking?

11 A. In the back yard.

12 Q. Is this statement of two pages the truth?

13 A. Yes.

14 Q. How have you been treated since your arrest?

15 A. Good.

16 Q. Have you made this two-page statement of your own

17 free will, without the use of force, fear, threats or

18 promises?

19 A. Yes.

20 Q. Have you read this statement before signing it?

21 A. --In the defendant's own handwriting, "Yes."

22 "Signature of Defendant, John H. Willman.

23 Witnesses, Detective Sergeant Charles McCurdy, Detective

24   Sergeant Michael Snider. "

25

ABOUT THE AUTHOR

Justin Dombrowski has studied local history for over fifteen years, specializing in local historical and criminal records. A native of Erie, Pennsylvania, he obtained a degree from Mercyhurst University and worked as an intern with the Erie County Detectives Unit. Having worked in the film industry since 2011, Justin is also a cofounder of Pickwick Entertainment, an independent film production company. His first book with The History Press, *Murder & Mayhem in Erie, Pennsylvania*, received critical acclaim for its writing and research. He resides in Erie, Pennsylvania.

Visit us at
www.historypress.com
···